PERIPLUS

Pocket
MALAY

Dictionary

Compiled by
Zuraidah Omar

D0089297

PERIPLUS

Published by Periplus Editions (HK) Ltd.

www.periplus.com

Copyright © 2002 Periplus Editions (HK) Ltd

ISBN 978-0-7946-0057-0

Distributed by:

Asia-Pacific
Berkeley Books Pte Ltd
61 Tai Seng Avenue #02-12
Singapore 534167
Tel: (65) 6280 1330; Fax: (65) 6280 6290
inquiries@periplus.com.sg; www.periplus.com

Indonesia
PT Java Books Indonesia
Jl. Rawa Gelam IV No. 9
Kawasan Industri Pulogadung
Jakarta 13930, Indonesia
Tel: 62 (21) 4682 1088; Fax: 62 (21) 461 0206
crm@periplus.co.id; www.periplus.com

North America, Latin America & Europe
Tuttle Publishing
364 Innovation Drive
North Clarendon, VT 05759-9436, USA
Tel: 1 (802) 773 8930; Fax: 1 (802) 773 6993
info@tuttlepublishing.com; www.tuttlepublishing.com

Japan
Tuttle Publishing
Yaekari Building 3rd Floor
5-4-12 Osaki, Shinagawa-ku
Tokyo 1410032, Japan
Tel: (81) 3 5437 0171; Fax: (81) 3 5437 0755
sales@tuttle.co.jp; www.tuttle.co.jp

18 17 16 15   12 11 10 9 8   1503CP

Printed in Singapore

Contents

Introduction iv

Pronunciation and Spelling Guide vi

Bahasa Malaysia–English Dictionary 1

English–Bahasa Malaysia Dictionary 47

Introduction

This Pocket Dictionary is an indispensable companion for visitors to Malaysia and for anyone in the early stages of learning Bahasa Malaysia or Malay, as it is commonly known. It contains the 3,000 or so Bahasa Malaysia words that are most frequently encountered in colloquial, everyday speech.

For the sake of clarity, only the common Bahasa Malaysia equivalents for each English word have been given. When an English word has more than one possible meaning, with different Bahasa Malaysia equivalents, each meaning is listed separately, with a clear explanatory gloss. The layout is clear and accessible, with none of the abbreviations and dense nests of entries typical of many small dictionaries.

Bahasa Malaysia is the official language of Malaysia, a country in which English, Chinese and Tamil are also widely spoken. There are numerous other languages, reflecting the diversity of the country's population.

Bahasa Malaysia is essentially a standardized form of Malay, originally found in the western part of the archipelago and spread via trade routes over the centuries. A slightly different form, with some variation in grammar and especially in vocabulary, is Bahasa Indonesia, the official language of Indonesia.

Malay has a rich history, and written records of Malay date from the 7th century CE in the form of inscriptions on the island of Sumatra. There was a flourishing literary tradition from the 14th century.

Malay/Indonesian is a member of the Western Austronesian group of languages. It is fairly closely related to Filipino, the national language of the Philippines based on the dominant local language Tagalog. It has more distant connections with New Zealand's Maori language and the other Eastern Austronesian languages of Hawaii, Fiji, Samoa and Tonga.

Bahasa Malaysia is written in two distinct scripts. The first, Jawi, is Arabic-based and was introduced into Malaysia by Muslim missionaries in the 15th century CE. Rumi, the second script, is the Roman alphabet, which came into being during the British administration. Unlike many other languages of Southeast Asia, Bahasa Malaysia is not tonal. Words do not have a heavy stress accent, and sentences should be pronounced smoothly and evenly. If there is a stress within a word, it falls on the second last syllable, never the last.

A striking characteristic of Bahasa Malaysia is the use of a system of verbal derivation. Derived forms of verbs are often made of root words plus prefixes and/or suffixes such as *mem-*, *ber-*, *-an* and *-i*, particularly in more formal speech and in written Bahasa Malaysia.

For instance, the word 'to take' in Bahasa Malaysia is *membawa* (made up of the root form *bawa* + the prefix *mem-*). However, for daily conversations, using only the root form is acceptable. Therefore, you could use the word *bawa* instead of *membawa* to translate 'to take'.

In this dictionary, verbs in Bahasa Malaysia are always listed alphabetically according to their simple root forms. This root is then followed by common affixed forms with the same meaning, if any. Complex verb forms with prefixes and suffixes attached are given only in cases where these are commonly found in colloquial speech.

A noun is sometimes made of a root form plus a prefix or suffix such as *me-*, *pe-* and *-an*, for example: root form *layan* 'to serve', *pelayan* (prefix *pe-*) 'person who serves (waiter, porter, etc.)', *pelayanan* (prefix *pe-*, suffix *-an*) 'service'. In this dictionary, nouns derived from root forms through the addition of prefixes and suffixes are always listed separately from their root words.

In contrast to this apparent complexity, from the point of view of speakers of English, Bahasa Malaysia is considerably simpler than many European languages in having no system of verbal tenses, no morphological plural forms, no verb 'to be' and no definite or indefinite articles. (Of course all of the associated concepts may be expressed in other ways: relative time is indicated by the use of adverbs such as *sudah* ('already'), *nanti* ('later'), *akan* ('will') and *belum* ('not yet'), the plural form is sometimes indicated by repeating the noun, and the addition of *-nya* to the end of a word gives a sense of definiteness.)

Many words in Bahasa Malaysia have been borrowed from English, and some of these are also included in this dictionary, even though they are easily understood by most speakers of English.

Pronunciation and Spelling Guide

To learn to pronounce the language correctly, ask a native speaker to read aloud some of the examples given in this section. Then try to imitate his or her pronunciation as accurately as you can. Be aware, however, that there are many dialectical variations in Bahasa Malaysia, some producing very strong accents. Stress also varies from region to region.

Unlike English, the spelling of Bahasa Malaysia is consistently phonetic. Many people say the pronunciation is similar to Spanish or Italian.

Consonants

Most are pronounced roughly as in English. The main exceptions are as follows:

c   is pronounced "ch" (formerly spelled "ch")
            cari   to look for, to seek   *cinta*   to love

g   is always hard, as in 'girl'
            guna   to use   *gila*   crazy

h   is very soft, and often not pronounced
            habis ⇒ *abis*   finished   *hidup* ⇒ *idup*   to live
            sudah ⇒ *suda*   already   *mudah* ⇒ *muda*   easy
            lihat ⇒ *liat*   to see   *tahu* ⇒ *tau*   to know

kh   is found in words of Arabic derivation, and sounds like a hard "k"
            khabar   news   *khusus*   special

ng   is always soft, as in 'hanger'
            dengar   to hear   *hilang*   lost

ngg   is always hard, as in 'hunger'
            ganggu   to bother   *mangga*   mango

r   is trilled or rolled, as in Spanish
            ratus   hundred   *baru*   new

sy   is pronounced "sh", as in 'shall'
            syarikat   company   *syarat*   condition

Vowels

As in English, there are five written vowels (a, e, i, o, u) and two diphthongs (ai, au):

a is very short, like the "a" in 'father'

    satu one   *bayar* to pay

e is usually unaccented, like the "u" in 'but'

    empat four   *beli* to buy

      When stressed, or at the end of a word, however, "e" sounds like the "é" in 'passé'

    dewan hall   *meja* table

i is long like the "ea" in 'bean'

    tiga three   *lima* five

o is long, as in 'so'

    bodoh stupid   *boleh* may

u is long like the "u" in 'humor'

    tujuh seven   *untuk* for

au is like the "ow" in 'how'

    atau or   *pulau* island

ai is pronounced like the word 'eye'

    pantai beach   *sampai* to reach

Bahasa Malaysia–English

A

abad century
abang older brother
abang angkat adopted brother, foster brother
abang ipar brother-in-law
abang tiri stepbrother
abah dad; daddy; father
abai neglect
abjad alphabet
abu ash
abuk, berabuk dust, dusty
acar pickled vegetables
acara program; event
ada to be; to exist; to have; to own
acab, beradab good manners; courteous; polite
adakalanya sometimes; occasionally
adat custom; tradition; culture
adat istiadat ceremony
adik younger brother or sister
adik-beradik brothers and sisters
adil just; fair
aduan, mengadu complaint, to complain
aduh! ouch!
agak guess
agama religion
agama Buddha Buddhism
agama Islam Islam
agama Kristian Christianity
agama Tao Taoism
agar in order that; so that

agas gnat
Ahad Sunday
agen agent
agensi agency
ahli member
air water
air masak boiled water
air mata tear (as in teardrop)
air minum drinking water
air panas hot spring
air terjun waterfall
ais ice
ais ice cream
ajaib baffling; miraculous
ajak, mengajak to invite; to ask along
ajal doom; death; ruin
ajar, mengajar to teach
ajuk, mengajuk mock; jeer; make fun of
akal mind
akan shall; will; would
akan tetapi however
akar root
akaun accounts
akhir last; end
akhirat eternity
akhirnya finally
akhir minggu end of week; weekend
akibat result; consequence
aku I (informal)
akui, mengakui to admit; to confess
alam nature
alamat address
alamat emel email address
alas meja tablecloth
alas piring tablemat

A

alasan excuse
alat tool; utensil; instrument
alat hawa dingin air conditioner
alat eletrik electrical appliance; electrical tool
alat tulis stationery
alir flow
alkohol alcohol; liquor; spirits
almari cupboard
am general
amalan practice
aman secure; safe
amanah, beramanah trust, trustworthy
amaran warning
amat very
ambil, mengambil take; fetch
ambulans ambulance
Amerika Syarikat America
ampun forgiveness; mercy
ampuni, mengampuni forgive
anak child
anak kapal sailor
anak lelaki son
anak perempuan daughter
anak saudara lelaki nephew
anak saudara perempuan niece
ancam, mengancam threaten
anda you (unfamilar, formal, polite)
andaian assumption
aneh strange ·
angan daydream
anggapan assumption
anggar, anggaran estimate, estimation
angguk nod one's head
anggun elegant
anggur grape
angin wind
angin taufan storm; typhoon
angka figure (number)
angkasa space; universe

angkat, mengangkat lift; raise up
angsa goose
aniaya abuse
anjing dog
anjung facade
anjur sponsor
ansuran instalment
antara among; between
antarabangsa international; between countries
antik antique
anting-anting earrings
anugerah award
apa? what?
apa khabar? how are you?
apa saja anything
apartmen apartment
api fire
apung float
arah direction
arahan instruction
arak alcohol; spirits; hard liquor
arang charcoal
artikel article
arus current (in body of water); flow of electricity
asah, mengasah sharpen, to sharpen
asal, berasal origin, to originate
asam sour; sharp taste like unripe fruit
asap smoke
asas basis
Asia Asia
asing foreign
askar soldier
asli indigenous; original
asrama hostel
atap roof
atas above; upstairs
atau or; either…or
atur, mengatur to arrange; to organize
awan cloud

awas! be careful!; look out!
ayah father
ayam chicken; poultry
ayam belanda turkey
ayam jantan cock; rooster
ayam panggang roast chicken
ayat sentence
ayuh come on; let's go
ayunan swing
azam determination
azan call to prayer (Muslim)

B

bab chapter
Baba Straits-born Chinese man
babi pig
baca, membaca read, to read
badam almond
badan body
bagai as; in the same degree
bagaikan as if
bagaimana? how?
bagaimanapun however
bagasi baggage
bagi give
bagus good; lovely (things)
bagus! well done!
bahagi divide; share
bahagia happy; blissful
bahagian bit (part)
bahagian yang dalam deep (location)
bahan material; ingredient
bahang heat; hot
bahas, berbahas debate
bahasa language
bahasa baku standard language
bahasa kebangsaan national language
bahasa rasmi official language
bahawa that
bahaya danger, dangerous
bahkan moreover; on the contrary

bahu shoulder
baik good; fine; lovely (person)
baik-baik be careful
baik...baik either...or
baju shirt; dress
baju dalam vest; undershirt
baju hujan raincoat
baju-t t-shirt
baju tidur nightdress; pajamas
baka heredity
bakal future
bakar, membakar burn; roast; toast
bakat talent; aptitude; flair
baki balance; remainder
bakti devote to a special purpose
bakul basket
balai hall; large room
balai polis police station
balai raya community hall
balak log of wood
balas, membalas answer (a letter); respond; retaliate
balasan reply; response
baldi bucket
baldu velvet
balik turn over; go back
baling throw; hurl
balu widow
balut wrap or cover on all sides
banci census
bancuh mix; stir together
bandar town
bandaran municipal
bandar raya city; main town
banding, dibanding compared to
bandingkan, membandingkan to compare to
banduan convict
bangga proud
bangkit evoke; get up; raise (an issue)
bangku bench
bangsa nationality; people

B

bangsal simple roofed farm building; cow shed
bangun, membangun awaken; build
bangunan building
banjir to be flooded; flood
bank bank
bantah, membantah disobey; object; protest
bantal pillow
bantal peluk bolster
bantu, membantu help
bantuan assistance; aid
banyak many; much
bapa father
bapa mentua father-in-law
bapa saudara uncle
barah cancer
baran rage; anger
barang thing; item; object
barang antik antiques
barang kemas jewelry
barang milik possession
barang peribadi personal belongings
barang pusaka inherited money or property
barang siapa anyone
barangan goods
barangkali probably; perhaps
barat west
barat daya southwest
barat laut northwest
baring recline; lie down
barisan queue; line
baru new
baru-baru just now; recently
bas bus
bas mini minibus
bas sekolah schoolbus
basah wet; damp
basah kuyup drenched; soaking wet
basahan something used daily (clothes)
basi stale; rotten; out-of-date
basikal bicycle

basuh wash (clothes)
batal, membatalkan cancel; invalidate
batang stick; pole
batas edge; boundary; limit
bateri battery
batin inner self; mental
batu stone; rock
batu giling roller for grinding spices
batuk cough
bau smell; odor (bad)
bau-bauan scent; fragrance
baucer voucher
bawa, membawa carry; bring
bawah below; downstairs
bawahan subordinate; inferior; of lower rank
bawang onion
bawang putih garlic
baya age
bayam spinach
bayang shadow; reflection
bayangkan, membayangkan imagine
bayar, membayar pay
bayaran payment
bayi baby
bazir, membazir spend recklessly; wasteful
beban burden; load
bebas free; unrestrained
bebel babbling talk
beberapa some; several
bebola daging meatball
beca trishaw
bedak powder
beg bag
beg baju suitcase
beg bimbit briefcase
beg duit purse
beg tangan handbag
begini thus; so; like this
begitu thus; so; like that
bekal cater or supply food; provide what is needed
bekas former; container

B

bekas bunga vase
bekerja to work
beku frozen
belacan prawn paste
belajar study; learn
belakang behind
Belanda Dutch
belang stripe
belanja buy; treat someone
belasan teen
beli, membeli buy
belia youth
beliau he/she
beluk turn
belukar bush
belum not yet
benang thread
benang bulu biri wool
benar true
benarkan allow; permit
bencana disaster
benci, membenci hate, to hate
benda object (thing)
bendera flag
bengkak swelling
bengkel garage (for repairs); workshop
bengkok bent; crooked
bentuk, membentuk shape, to form
benua continent
beracun poisonous
berak shit; defecate
berangkat depart
berani brave
berapa? how many/much?
berapa lama? how long?
beras uncooked rice
berat heavy
berbagai-bagai all sorts; various
berbahasa polite; well mannered; cultured
berbaik be on good terms
berbintik-bintik spotted (pattern)

bercorak patterned
berdiri stand, to stand up
beres solved; arranged; okay
berbaris stand in line; queue
bergaris-garis striped
bergurau tease
berharga of worth
berhasil achieve desired result
berhenti stop; cease
beri, memberi give; present
berikut next; following
berikutnya the next; the following
berita news
beritahu inform
berjalan-jalan to travel
berjanji to promise
berjaya to succeed
berjenaka to joke
berjumlah altogether; in total
berkelakuan baik well-behaved
berkeliling to go around
berkembang to develop; to expand; to grow up (child)
berkilat shiny
berlawak to joke
bermurah hati generous
bernilai to be worth
berpendapat to think (have an opinion)
berpisahan apart; to be separated
bersalah wrong; guilty
bersama together
berseronok to have fun
bersih clean
bersin sneeze
bersulam embroidered
bersyarah to make a speech
bersyukur grateful
bertambah berat to gain weight
bertengkar to quarrel
bertolak to depart
berubah to change
beruntung lucky

B

berus brush
berus gigi toothbrush
besar big; large
besar sekali huge
besen basin
beserta together with
besi metal; iron
betis calf (of leg)
betul true; correct; repaired
betulkan, membetulkan repair; fix
beza, berbeza differ; to be different; difference
biarkan, membiarkan allow; let alone; leave be
biasa usual; regular; normal
bibir lips
bicara, berbicara speak; talk
bidan midwife
bidang scope; range of a subject; domain
bijak, bijaksana reasonable (sensible); wise
biji seed
biji bijan sesame seeds
bijiran cereal
bikin, membikin make
bil bill
bila when
bila saja whenever
bilang say; count
bilangan number
bilik room (in a house)
bilik air bathroom
bilik darjah classroom
bilik makan dining room
bilik mandi bathroom
bilik tidur bedroom
bilion billion
bimbang worry
bina, membina build
binasa, membinasa destroy; perish
binatang animal
binatang peliharaan pet animal
bincang, berbincang discuss

bingung, membingungkan puzzled; confused, confusing, to confuse
bini wife
bintang star
bintik spot; fleck
bir beer
biri-biri sheep
biro bureau
biru blue
bisik; berbisik whisper
bising noisy; loud
biskut sweet biscuit; cookie
biskut kraker crackers
bisu mute; silent
bisul boil; inflamed swelling with pus
blaus blouse
blok block of a building
bocor leak; have a hole
bodoh stupid; ignorant
bogel nude
bohong make up a story; tell a (white) lie
bola ball
bola jaring netball
bola keranjang basketball
bola sepak football
boleh able to; can; allowed to
boleh jadi possible; maybe
bomba fire brigade
bomoh medicine man
bonda mother
bongkak arrogant; overbearing; boastful
bongkar break apart; unpack; disassemble
bonjol bulge; rounded swelling
borang form
boros extravagant
bosan to be bored
botak bald
botol bottle
bra bra
brek brake
British British
brokoli broccoli

buah fruit
buah dada breast
buah pinggang kidney
bual, berbual converse
buang, membuang cast out; throw away
buang air besar defecate
buang air kecil urinate
buas savage; wild and fierce
buat, berbuat, membuat do; make; produce; prepare
buatan product of; artificial
buat apa? what for?
buaya crocodile
bubur porridge
budak child
budak lelaki boy; male child
budak perempuan girl; female child
budaya, kebudayaan culture
budi kindness; good deed
bujang single (not married)
bujur oblong
buka, membuka open
buka baju take off clothes; get undressed
bukaan opening; aperture
bukan not; none
bukit hill
bukti proof
buku book
buku catatan notebook
buku harian diary; journal
buku lali ankle
bulan month; moon
bulanan monthly
bulat round (shape)
bulatan circle
bulu fur
bulu kening eyebrow
bulu mata eyelash
bumbung roof
bumi Earth
buncis green beans
bunga flower; interest (on loan)
bunga api fireworks
bungkus wrap into a bundle

bungkusan package; parcel
buntut rear; tail; buttocks
bunuh, membunuh kill
bunyi, berbunyi sound; noise
bunyikan to make a sound with something (e.g. bell)
buru hunt
buruh labor
buruk ugly; bad
burung bird
busuk rotten; off (gone bad)
buta blind
butir point; fact; a detail

C

cabang branch
cabar, mencabar to challenge
cabaran challenge
cabut pull out; to flee
cabut lari to take off; to leave immediately
cabutan draw (lucky draw)
cacak upright
cacar smallpox
cacat defect; handicap
cacat akal mentally challenged
caci scorn; abuse
cacing worm
cadang, bercadang intend
cadangan proposal; suggestion
cadar bedsheet
cagar, cagaran deposit
cahaya light
cair thin (of liquids)
cakap, bercakap speak; talk
cakap besar boastful; brag
cakap kosong talk nonsense
cakar claw
cakera padat compact disc
calar scratch
calon candidate
cam, mengecam recognize; identify someone
camca spoon

C

camca teh teaspoon
campak throw; fling; hurl
campur mixed; to mix
campur tangan interfere; get involved in; meddle
campuran combination; mixture
candi Hindu temple; shrine
candu opium
canggih sophisticated
cangkuk hook onto something
cangkul hoe
cantik beautiful (of women)
cantum combine; join together
cap brand; stamp; print
cap jari fingerprint
capai, mencapai reach; attain
capal sandals
capik lame; limp
cara way of doing things; method
cari, mencari look for; search
carta chart; map
caruman subscription; fee; contribution
carut obscene language
cat paint
cat air water colors
cat minyak oil paint
catat, mencatat note down
catatan notes
catur chess
cawan cup
cawangan branch (of a bank)
cawat loin cloth
cebis bit; piece
cebisan small piece or quantity
cebis bit; piece
cebok water dipper
cedera injure
cedok, mencedok scoop up
cegah prohibit; prevent
cek cheque
cekap skillful; efficient
cekik strangle

celak eye liner
celik open (eyes)
celup dip; dye
celur scald
cemas frightened; desperate
cemburu jealous; envious; envy
cemerlang excellent
cencaluk prawn pickle
cendawan mushroom
cenderamata souvenir
cenderung inclined towards; have preference for
cendul drink of jelly-like strips of dough and coconut milk
cengkam grasp; grip; clutch
cengkih clove
cepat fast; quick
cerah clear (of weather); sunny
cerai divorce; scatter
ceramah lecture; talk
cerdik clever
cerek kettle
cerewet fussy; fastidious
cergas energetic; alert
cerita story
cerita karut cock-and-bull story
cerita rakyat folklore
cermat careful; cautious
cermin, mencerminkan mirror; to reflect
cermin mata spectacles
ceroboh trespass
ceruk corner; secluded place
cerut cigar
cetak, mencetak print; publish
cetak rompak piracy (of books, music, movies)
cetakan edition; print
cetek shallow
ceti money lender
cetus outburst; outbreak
cicak lizard
cicit great grandchild
cicir dropping; falling
Cik Miss

D

cikgu teacher
cili chili
Cina Chinese
cincin ring (jewelry)
cinta, mencintai love; to love
cipta, mencipta create
ciptaan creation
ciri characteristic
cirit-birit diarrhoea
cita-cita ambition
cium, mencium kiss;
  smell (something with nose)
cocok fitting; suitable;
  appropriate
cogan kata slogan
coklat brown
comel cute; tiny
comot dirty; grubby
conteng doodle; scribble
contoh sample; example
corak pattern; design
corong funnel; chimney
cuaca weather
cuaca yang kurang
  bagus/cerah dull weather
cuai careless; negligent
cuba, mencuba try;
  try on (clothes)
cubaan attempt
cubit, mencubit pinch
cuci, mencuci wash;
  develop (a roll of film)
cuci piring wash dishes
cucu grandchild
cucu lelaki grandson
cucu perempuan
  granddaughter
cucuk pin; inject; prick; pierce
cucuk sanggul hair pin
cuit touch playfully
cuka vinegar
cukai tax
cukai pendapatan income tax
cukup enough
cukup bulan end of the month
cukup umur be of age
cukur shave

cuma merely; only
cungkil, mencungkil dig out;
  extract
curah pour
curahan downpour; outpour
curam steep
curang cheat (in a relationship);
  dishonest
curi, mencuri steal
curiga suspect
cuti leave; holiday; vacation
cuti am public holiday
cuti sakit medical leave

D

dacing scale
dada chest
dadah drug
daerah region; district
daftar register; a list
daging meat
daging ayam chicken meat
daging babi pork
daging biri-biri mutton; lamb
daging kambing goat meat
daging lembu beef
dagu chin
dahaga thirsty
dahan branch of a tree
dahi forehead
dahsyat terrible; horrible
dahulu former; before; past
dahulu kala long time ago
dakwa accuse
dakwah, berdakwah sermon;
  preach
dakwat ink
dalam inside; deep
dalang puppeteer
damai peace
damping intimate (friendship);
  close
dan and
dana funds
dandan do one's hair

D

dapat, mendapat get; reach; attain; succeed; to be able
dapur kitchen
dapur eletrik electric oven
dapur gas gas stove
darah blood
darat, mendarat land; to land
dari from (place); of
daripada from (person); than; instead of
dari mana? where did you just come from?
darjat degree
darurat emergency
dasar basis
datang arrive; come
datang bulan menstruate; period
datar flat (smooth)
dataran plains (level ground)
Datin title of distinction for the wife of a Datuk
Dato', Datuk title of distinction bestowed upon a man or woman
datuk grandfather
datuk nenek grandparents
daun leaf
daun saderi celery
dawai wire
daya force; power; capacity
daya berfikir thinking power
daya cipta creative ability
daya upaya ability
debu dust
dedah make known
degil stubborn
dekah laugh loudly
dekan college dean
dekat near
dekati, mendekati to approach
demam fever
demam panas high fever
demi for
demikian hence; therefore
demikian juga likewise

denda fine (punishment)
dendam revenge; grudge
dengan with
dengan cepat quickly
dengar, mendengar hear
dengarkan, mendengarkan listen to
denggi dengue
dengki jealous; envy
dengkur, berdengkur snore
depan front; next
deposit to deposit (money)
deras swift
deret row; line
derita suffering
derma donation
desa country (rural area)
desak urge; push
dewan hall
Dewan Negara Senate
Dewan Rakyat House of Representatives
dewasa adult
di in; at; on
di- (used in the passive form of verbs)
di atas on top of; above; upstairs
di bawah below; underneath; downstairs
di depan in front of; at the front; opposite
di jalan on the road
di luar outside; outside of
di mana? where?
di mana-mana everywhere
di muka in front of; at the front
di rumah at home
di samping beside
di sana over there (far away)
di situ over there
dia he; she; it; him; her
diagonal diagonal
dialek dialect
diam, berdiam silent; to be silent

diam-diam secretly; quietly
diawetkan cured; preserved (foods and other goods)
dibahagi to divide
dibandingkan dengan compared with
didih, mendidih boil
didik, mendidik educate
didinginkan chilled
dilarang forbidden
dinding wall
dingin cold
dipanggil called (name)
diri, berdiri self; to stand
diraja royal
dirikan, mendirikan to build; to establish
diskaun discount
disket diskette
doa prayer
dobi laundry
dodoi lullaby
dodol Malay delicacy
doktor general practitioner
doktor bedah surgeon
doktor gigi dentist
dompet wallet; purse
dongeng legend
dorong, mendorong push; urge; encourage
dorongan encouragement
dosa sin
dozen dozen
drebar driver; chauffeur
dua two
dua belas twelve
dua kali ganda double (two times)
dua puluh twenty
dubur anus
duda widower
duduk sit
duduk-duduk sit around
duga guess
dugaan conjecture
duit money
duit kecil small change

duit kopi bribe
duit syiling coin
dukacita sorry; unhappy
dukun medicine man
dukung, mendukung carry; support
dulang tray
dulu first; beforehand; in the past
dunia world
duta ambassador; emissary
dusun orchard
duti duty (tax)
duti kastam customs duty

E

edaran cycle
eja, mengeja spell (words)
ejaan spelling
ejek, mengejek mock; jeer
ejekan mockery
ekar acre
ekonomi economy
ekor tail
ekoran consequence
ekspedisi expedition
eksport, mengeksport export
ekspres express
ekzos exhaust (in car)
ela yard (measurement)
elak, mengelak avoid; dodge
elastik elastic
elaun allowance
eletrik electric
elektronik electronic
elok beautiful; good
emak mother
emak mertua mother-in-law
emak saudara aunt
emas gold
embun dew; mist
e-mel email
emosi emotion
empat four
empat belas fourteen

E

E

empat puluh forty
empuk soft
enak tasty
enam six
enam belas sixteen
enam puluh sixty
Encik Mr
enggan refuse; reluctant
engkau you (familiar, friend, same status)
enjin engine
entah don't know
epal apple
erat closely related; connected
Eropah Europe
erti, bererti meaning; to mean
eskalator escalator
esok tomorrow

F

faedah benefit
faham understand
fahaman understanding
fail file
fajar dawn
fajar menyinsing at break of dawn
fakir poor; pauper
faks fax (machine)
fakta fact
fakulti faculty (in college or university)
faraj vagina
farmasi pharmacy; drugstore
fasa phase
fasal clause (in a contract)
fasih fluent
feri ferry
fesyen fashion
fikir, berfikir think; to think
fikiran thought; idea; opinion
fiksyen fiction
filem film (movie, camera)
Filipina the Philippines
firma firm (business)

fitnah slander; libel
fius fuse
foto photograph
fotostat photostat
fungsi function

G

gabung to join together
gadai pawn
gading ivory; tusk
gadis girl
gado-gado vegetable salad with peanut sauce
gaduh, bergaduh uproar; to fight
gagah strong; dashing
gagak crow
gagal fail
gagap stammer
gajah elephant
gaji wages; salary
gajus cashew nut
galah pole
galak encourage
gali, menggali dig
galian mineral
gam gum
gamam, tergamam stunned
gambar picture; drawing; image
gambaran impression
gambarkan, menggambarkan to draw; to describe
gambar rajah diagram
ganas violent
ganda double
ganding, berganding alongside; close beside
gandum wheat
ganggu, mengganggu disturb; bother; disrupt
gangguan disturbance
gangsa bronze
ganja marijuana
ganjaran reward

ganjil unusual; odd (number)
ganti, menggantikan change; replace; switch
ganti spare (part, tyre)
ganti rugi indemnity
gantung hang; suspend
garaj garage
garam salt
garang fierce
garau hoarse
garing crisp
garis line
garpu fork
garu rake; scratch
gasing top
gatal itch
gaul mix; associate with
gaung ravine; chasm
gaya style; manner
gayung ladle; dipper
gebar blanket
gebu soft; fluffy
gedung serbanika department store
gegar shaking
gegaran jarring movement
gegat moth
gelak laugh
gelak ketawa laughter
gelang kaki anklet
gelang tangan bracelet
gelanggang arena
gelap dark
gelap gelita pitch dark
gelaran title
gelas glass
gelebar flapping
gelecek slip; lose balance
geledah search; ransack
gelek, menggelek roll over
gelembung bubble
gelen gallon
geleng shake one's head
gelesek rubbing
geletar tremble; shiver
geletek tickle
geli amused; ticklish

geli hati amused
gelimpang sprawled
gelincir, menggelincir slip; fall down
gelisah anxious; worried; restless
gelobor baggy; hanging loosely
gelojoh greedy
gelombang wave; wavelength
gelongsor slide
gema echo
gemar fancy; be a fan of
gembira, mengembirakan excited; happy; rejoicing
gementar tremble
gemilang brilliant; glorious
gempa bumi earthquake
gempal chubby; plump
gemuk fat; stout
genap complete
gendang drum
genggam grasp
genit cute; petite
genting gap in mountain
genyeh, menggenyeh rub
gerabak coach of a train
gerai stall
gerak, bergerak move
gerakan movement; action
gerak-gerik movements
gerak hati intuition
gerak laku behavior
geram angry; annoyed
geran grant
gerbang gate
gereja church
gergaji saw
gerhana eclipse
gerimis drizzle
gerobok cupboard
gertak threat
gerun frightened
getah rubber
getar, bergetar jolt; move jerkily
ghaib supernatural

G

ghairah passion
giat active
gigi teeth
gigil, menggigil shiver
gigit, mengigit bite
gila crazy; insane
gilang-gemilang glittering
giling, menggiling grind
gila crazy; insane
gilap polish; burnish
gilir take turns; alternate
giliran turn
gincu lipstick
ginjal kidney
girang cheerful; joyful
gitar guitar
goda tempt; entice
golek roll
golf golf
golongan class; category
goncang, bergoncang shake
gopoh-gapah hastily
goreng fried
gores scratch
gosok scrub; brush; iron
gotong-royong cooperative
  undertaking or effort
goyang swing; shake
graduan graduate
gred grade
gua cave
gubah, menggubah arrange;
  compose
gubahan composition
gudang godown; warehouse
gugur wilt; fall (leaves);
  die prematurely (in battle,
  before birth)
gula sugar
gula-gula confectionery;
  candy; sweets
gula merah brown sugar
gulai gravy
guli marble
guling rotate
gulung roll
guna, berguna useful

gunakan, menggunakan make
  use of
guni jute bag
gunting scissors
guntingan clipping
gunung mountain
gunung api volcano
gurau joke
gurauan banter
gurau senda lighthearted
  action; amusing incident
guru teacher
guru besar headmaster;
  school principal
guruh thunder
gurun desert (arid land)
gusi gum (of mouth)
gusti wrestle

H

haba heat
habis gone; finished
habiskan, menghabiskan
  finish off
habuk dust
had limit
had laju speed limit
hadap, menghadapi face;
  confront
hadapan in front
hadiah gift
hadiah sagu hati consolation
  prize
hadir to attend; present (here)
hadirin attendees
hafaz memorize
haid menstruate; period
hairan astonish; amaze
haiwan animal
Hajah woman who has made
  pilgrimage to Mecca
hajat purpose; intention
Haji man who has made
  pilgrimage to Mecca
hak right

H

hak asasi manusia human rights

hak cipta copyright

hakim judge

hal topic; matter

hal ehwal affairs

hala direction

halal permissible (according to Islamic law)

halaman compound

halia ginger

hal kecil minor (not important); small matter

halaman page; compound

halang bar (the way); obstruct

halangan obstacle

halau, menghalau chase away

haluan direction; course

halus refined; well-mannered

halwa preserved fruits in syrup

hama germ

hambar bland

hambat, menghambat chase; to chase

hamil pregnant

hampa disappointed

hampa beras rice husk

hampir almost; nearly

hampir tidak barely; hardly

hancing bad smell; stinking

hancur destroyed; dissolved

handal successful; clever

hangat warm

hangit burning smell

hangus burnt; scorched

hantam hit hard

hantar, menghantar deliver

hantaran something that is delivered; dowry

hantu ghost

hantuk knock against

hanya only

hanyut washed away

hapak musty smell

hapus wipe out; abolish

haram unlawful; forbidden

harap, berharap to hope

harapkan, mengharapkan expect, to expect

harapan hope; expectation

harga cost

harga diri pride in oneself

harga jualan selling price

harga mati fixed price

hari day

hari bulan date

hari depan in future

hari ini today

hari kelepasan public holiday

hari lahir birthday

harian daily

harimau tiger

harta property

hartawan wealthy person

harum sweet smell

haruman fragrance; perfume

harus necessary; have to

hasil result; produce

hasil bumi natural resources

hasrat desire

hati liver

hati-hati! be careful!; cautious

haus thirsty

hawa climate

hayat life

hebat great; formidable; impressive

heboh noisy

helai piece (of cloth)

helo hello; hi

hemat careful; frugal

hembus blow

hendak intend to; want

henti, berhenti stop

heran surprised

hias decorate

hiasan ornament; decoration

hiasan kepala headdress

hibur entertain

hidangan dish (particular food)

hidung nose

hidup live

hijau green

hilang lose; lost

hilangkan, menghilangkan get rid of
hinaan, menghina insult
hingga until
hiris, menghiris slice; cut
hirup, menghirup sip; suck
hisap, menghisap suck
hitam black
hitung count
hodoh ugly
hormat respect
hubungan connection
hubung contact
hujan rain; to be raining
hujan lebat heavy rain
hujung tip; point; end
hujung jalan end of the road
hukum law
huruf character (written)
hutan forest; jungle
hutang owe (money); debt

imbang equal; balanced
imigresen immigration
import, mengimport import
indah beautiful (of things, places)
ingat, mengingat remember
ingatkan, mengingatkan remind
ingin, berkeinginan wish
ini this
intan diamond
inti essence; core
invois invoice
ipar in-law
iri envy; envious; jealous
isi, mengisi fill
Isnin Monday
isteri wife
istimewa special
itik duck
itu that

I

ia (= dia) he; she; it
ibu mother
ibu jari thumb
ibu kota capital city (of state)
ibu mentua mother-in-law
ibu negara capital city (of country)
ibu saudara aunt
idea idea
ijazah university degree
ikan fish
ikan masin salted fish
ikan yu shark
ikat jamin bail
ikat tie; handwoven textile
ikhlas sincere
iklan advertisement
iklim climate
ikut, mengikut follow along; go along
ilmu knowledge

J

jabatan department (in a company)
jadi, menjadi therefore; to become
jadual schedule; timetable
jaga, menjaga guard
jagaan supervision; custody
jaguh champion
jagung corn
jagung manis sweetcorn
jahat wicked; bad
jahit, menjahit sew
jaja, menjaja hawk goods
jaket jacket; coat
jala fishing net
jalan walk; function; street; road
jalan-jalan go out; go walking
jalanraya highway
jalan kaki walk on foot
jalan mati dead-end street
jalan sehala one-way street

jalur band; stripe
jam hour; o'clock
jambak bouquet
jamban toilet; lavatory
jambatan bridge
jamin, menjamin guarantee; assure
jaminan guarantee; assurance
jampi magical spells
jamuan feast; banquet
janda widow; widowed
jangan do not!
jangan buat begitu! don't do it!
jangan nakal! don't be naughty; behave!
janggut beard
jangka period (of time)
jangkamasa duration
jangkit, berjangkit infect; infectious
janji, berjanji promise; to make a promise
jantina gender
jantung heart
jarak distance
jarang transparent; rarely seen
jarang-jarang rarely; seldom
jari finger(s)
jari kaki toe(s)
jaring net
jarum needle
jasa service
jati genuine; authentic
jatuh fall
jatuhkan, menjatuhkan drop
jatuh cinta fall in love
jauh far
jawab, menjawab answer; reply
jawapan answer; response
jawatan post; job
jawatankuasa committee
jaya, berjaya successful; succeed
jejak footstep
jejambat overhead bridge

jejantas flyover
jelajah, menjelajah explore
jelak fed up; bored with
jelang, menjelang eve; approaching
jelas, menjelaskan make clear; clarify
jelik ugly
jelita lovely; pretty
jem jam
jemput, menjemput pick someone up; invite
jemputan invitation
jemput-jemput dumpling made of flour and banana
jemu bored; tired of something
jemur dry out
jenaka, berjenaka banter; joke
jenama brand
jenayah crime
jendela window
jenis type; sort
jentera machinery
Jepun Japan
jerang, menjerang boil (water)
jerebu haze
jerit, menjerit shout
Jerman German
jernih pure; clear
jeruk pickle
jerung shark
jeti jetty
jijik disgusting
jika, jikalau if; when
jilat, menjilat lick
jimat thrifty
jinak tame
jingga orange (color)
jintan manis aniseed
jintan putih cumin
jiran neighbor
jirus pour over with water
jiwa soul
joget dance
johan champion
jolok, menjolok poke; thrust
jorong oval (shape)

J

jual, menjual sell
jualan murah cheap sale
juara champion
jubah long dress
jubin tile
judi, berjudi gamble
judul title of book or article
juga also; as well; likewise
jujur honest
Jumaat Friday
jumlah amount; total
jumpa, berjumpa, menjumpai meet
jumpaan discovery
junjung, menjunjung carry on the head
juntai, berjuntai dangle; dangling
jurujual salesperson
jururawat nurse
juruwang cashier
jus juice
juta million
jutawan millionaire

K

kabel cable
kabus fog; mist
kaca glass; mirror
kacak handsome
kacamata eyeglasses; spectacles
kacang bean; peanut
kacang hitam black beans
kacang pis peas
kacau disturbed; messy; disorderly
kad card
kadang-kadang sometimes; occasionally
kadar rate
kadar pertukaran exchange rate
kadbod cardboard
kaedah method

kahwin, berkahwin marry
kain cloth; fabric; textile
kaitan relevance
kajian study
kakak older sister
kaki leg; foot (measurement)
kakitangan staff
kaki lima covered walk along side of shops
kaku stiff
kalah lose; defeated
kalahkan, mengalahkan to defeat
kalau if; when; what about?; how about?
kalau tidak or else (do something or else)
kali times
kalkulator calculator
kalung necklace
kambing goat
Kemboja Cambodia
kamera camera
kami we (excluding the addressee); our (when following object)
kampung village; hamlet
kampus campus
kamu you (familiar, friend, same status)
kamus dictionary
Kanada Canada
kanak-kanak child
kanan right (opposite of left)
kandung, mengandungi contain; consist of
kangkung a kind of spinach
kanji starch
kanta lens
kantin canteen
kapak axe
kapal ship
kapal terbang aeroplane
kapas cotton
kapur chalk
karang, mengarang coral; to write

karangan article; essay
karat, berkarat rust; rusty
karot carrot
kartun cartoon
karut nonsense
karya masterpiece
kasar coarse; rude
kaset cassette
kasih love; affection
kasihan pity
kasut shoe
kata, berkata word; to say
katak frog
katil bed
kaunter counter
kawan friend
kawasan region
kawat wire
kahwin to be married
kaya rich; wealthy
kayu wood
kayuh pedal (bicycle)
ke to; towards
ke mana saja anywhere
ke suatu tempat to have been somewhere
keadaan situation (how things are)
keadaan sekeliling surroundings
keadaan sekitar surroundings
keadilan justice
kebanggaan pride; elation
kebangsaan nationality
kebanyakan most
kebebasan freedom
kebencian hatred
keberangkatan departure
keberanian bravery
keberatan to mind (be displeased)
kebersihan cleanliness
kebetulan actually; as it happens; really (in fact)
kebiasaan used to (accustomed)
kebudayaan culture

kebuluran famine
kebun garden
kebun bunga botanical gardens
kicap (manis) (sweet) soy sauce
kecantikan beauty
kecederaan injury
kecekapan efficiency
kecemaran udara air pollution
kecemasan emergency; dread
kecewa disappointed; upset
kecil small
kecil sekali tiny; very small
kecuali except for; unless
kecurian burglary; theft
kecut shrunken
kedai shop
kedekut stingy
kedut crease
kedutaan embassy
kedua second
kegiatan activity
kehadiran attendance
kehangatan warmth (temperature)
kchormatan honor
kejadian incident; occurrence
kejam harsh; cruel
kejar, mengejar chase
keju cheese
kejut, terkejut surprised; startled
kek cake
kekasih lover
kelabu gray
kelah, berkelah picnic; go on a picnic
kelahiran birth
kelakar funny; amusing
kelakuan behavior
kelambatan delayed (late)
kelambu mosquito net
kelamin sex; gender
kelapa coconut
kelaparan hungry
kelas class

K

kelasi sailor
kelawar bat
kelayakan qualification
kelebaran width
keledek yam
kelihatannya to look (seem, appear)
keliling around
kelilingi, mengelilingi encircle; to go around
kelip-kelip firefly
keliru confused
kelompok group; batch
keluar go out; exit
keluarga family; relatives
keluarkan, mengeluarkan to put out (money)
keluh, mengeluh to sigh
keluhan sigh
kemalangan accident
kemaluan lelaki penis
kemaluan perempuan vagina
kemarahan anger
kemarau dry (of weather); drought
kemarin the day before yesterday
kemas tidy
kematian death
kembali return; go back
kembang blossom
kembangkan, mengembangkan to expand
kembar twin
kemewahan affluence; wealth
kemudahan amenity; facility
kemudian then; afterwards
kemuncak summit
kemungkinan possibility
kena to be hit; incur
kenaikan increase
kenal, mengenal know; recognize; be acquainted
kenalan acquaintance
kenang-kenangan souvenir
kenangan memories
kenapa? why?; what for?

kencing urinate
kendaraan motor vehicle
kendi jug (pitcher)
kentang potato
kentut fart
kenyang full (having eaten enough)
kenyataan statement
kepada to; toward (a person)
kepak wing
kepala head
kepercayaan beliefs; faith
keputusan decision
kera ape; monkey
kerajaan government
keramahan warmth (personal characteristic)
keramat sacred
kerana because
keranjang basket
kerap frequent
keras hard; firm (mattress)
kerat cut
kerbau water buffalo
kereta car
kereta api train
kereta peronda patrol car (police)
kereta sorong cart
keretek clove cigarette
kering dry
kerja, bekerja work
kerjasama cooperation
kertas paper
kerongkong throat
kerosakan damage
kerusi chair
kerusi tangan armchair
kesal regret
kesalahan, menyalahkan error; fault; mistaken; to blame
kesal regret
kesan impression; effect
kesedaran awareness
keseluruhan entirety; whole

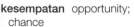

K

kesempatan opportunity; chance
kesemutan numb; gone to sleep (leg, arm); pins and needles
kesimpulan conclusion
kesusasteraan literature
ketam crab
ketat tight
ketawa laugh
keterangan information
ketiga third
ketinggalan to miss (bus, flight)
ketinggian height
ketua chief; leader
ketuk knock
ketumbar coriander (cilantro)
keturunan descendant
khabar news
Khamis Thursday
khas special
khuatir afraid; worry
khusus special
kilang factory
kilat lightning
kilogram kilogram
kilometer kilometer
kini nowadays; presently
kipas fan
kipas angin electric fan
kira, mengira guess; suppose; count
kira-kira approximately; roughly
kiri left
kirim, mengirim send
kirim surat, mengirim surat send mail
kita we (includes the addressee); our (when placed after an object)
klinik clinic
kobis cabbage
koyak tear (in fabric)
kolam pool
kolam renang swimming pool

kolera cholera
komputer computer
kongsi share
kopi coffee
korban sacrifice
Korea Selatan South Korea
Korea Utara North Korea
kos cost
kosong empty; nought; zero
kot coat
kot panjang overcoat
kota city; town; downtown; urban area
kotak box
kotor dirty
kotoran stain
kraf tangan handicraft
krim cream
Kristian Christian
kuah broth; gravy
kuala confluence (of river)
kuali frying pan with round bottom (wok)
kuasa power; authority
kuat strong; energetic
kuatkuasa enforce
kubu fortress
kubur grave
kuburan gravesite
kucar-kacir in a mess
kucing cat
kuda horse
kueh cake; pastry; cookie
kueh bola dumpling
kugiran musical group
kuil temple
kuku fingernail
kukuh firmly fixed
kukus steamed
kulat fungus
kulit skin; leather
kuman germ; bacteria
kumpul gather
kumpulan group
kumur, berkumur rinse the mouth
kunci key; lock

K

kuning yellow
kunjungan a visit
kunjungi visit
kuno ancient
kuntum flower bud
kunyah, mengunyah chew
kunyit turmeric
kupon coupon
kupas, mengupas peel
kupu-kupu butterfly
kura-kura turtle
kurang less; lacking; minus
kurangi, mengurangi reduce
kurang nasib baik unlucky
kurang pasti uncertain
kurang senang unhappy;
   upset
kurnia give an award
kursus course
kurun century
kurung, mengurung confine
kurus thin; slim; slender
kusut dishevelled
kusyen cushion
kutip, mengutip pick; collect

L

labah-labah spider
labuh hanging down (long
   dress)
labur invest
laci drawer
lada pepper; chili
lada hitam black pepper
lada putih white pepper
ladang field; estate
laga, berlaga fight head on
lagi more; again; another
lagipun besides (in any case)
lagu song
lahir, dilahirkan born;
   to be born
lahirkan, melahirkan to give
   birth
lain different

laju speed; fast
laki husband
lakon act
lakonan play; drama
laku, berlaku sold; valid;
   to be valid; to take place
lakukan, melakukan to do
lalai careless
lalang tall grass
lalat fly
lalu past; then; to pass
laluan the way through
lalu-lalang back and forth
lalu-lintas traffic
lama old (of things); a long
   time
lama-lama in the end
lama-kelamaan finally
laman dalam courtyard
lambai wave
lambat slow; late
lambat-laun sooner or later
lambung, melambung toss in
   the air; bounce
lampin diaper
lampir, melampirkan attach;
   affix; enclose
lampu light; lamp
lampu picit flashlight
lancar smooth; proficient;
   fluent
lancong, melancong tour;
   travel
landasan kereta api railroad;
   railway
langgan, berlanggan
   subscribe
langganan subscription
langit sky
langkah step
langsing slender; slim
langsir curtain
langsung directly; non-stop
lantai floor
lap, mengelap wipe or clean
   with cloth
lapan eight

L

apan belas eighteen
apan puluh eighty
apang spacious
apangan terbang airport; airfield
apar hungry
apis layer
apor, melapor report
aporan a report
apuk mouldy; stale
aram, melaram stylish; showing off
arang, melarang forbid; prevent
ari run; escape
aris selling well
asak durable
atarbelakang background to a story or report
atihan practice; training
auk cooked food
aut sea
awak joke
awan oppose; opponent; rival
awat, melawat visit
ayak qualified
ayan, melayani serve (food, etc.)
ayanan service (in a restaurant)
ayang-layang kite
ayar, berlayar a sail; to sail
ayu withered
azat delicious; tasty
azim habitual; usual
ebah bee
ebam bruise
ebar wide; width
ebat dense; thick
ebih more
ebih banyak more of
ebih buruk worse
ebih kurang more or less
ebih suka prefer
ebuh avenue; street
eceh slow; troublesome

lecur scalded
lega feel relieved
leher neck
lekas quick; fast
lekas sembuh get well soon
lekat stick
lekit, melekit sticky
lelah tired; weary; asthma
lelap sound asleep
lelaki male
lelong auction off
lemah weak
lemah hati soft-hearted
lemah lembut graceful
lemah semangat weak-willed
lemak fat
lembab damp; humid
lembah valley
lembik soft; flaccid
lembu cow
lembut gentle
lempar, melempar throw
lempeng type of pancake
lempuk cake made from durian and sugar
lemon lemon
lena sound asleep
lencana badge
lencong, melencong deviate
lencongan detour; deviation
lendir something sticky and slimy
lengah dawdle
lengan arm
lengan baju sleeve
lengkap complete
lentuk bend
lenyap disappear; vanish
lepak lounge about lazily
lepas release; let go
lerengan slope
lesap disappear; vanish
lesen licence
lesu listless; fatigue
letak, meletak place; put
leter, meleter nag
letih tired; weary; worn out

L

letup, meletup blow up; explode
letusan eruption
lewat late
liar wild
liat not easily cut; hard
libat, melibat involve
licin smooth; slippery
lidah tongue
lif elevator
liga league
lihat, melihat see; look; observe
lihatlah! look!
lilin candle; wax
lima five
lima belas fifteen
lima puluh fifty
limau lemon (citrus)
limau nipis lime
limpa liver
limpah overflow, overflowing
lindung protect
lingkaran circle; spiral
lingkungan environment
lintas, melintas cross (the road)
lipan centipede
lipas cockroach
lipat, melipat fold
lobak merah carrot
loceng bell
logam metal
loghat dialect
lokek stingy; miserly
loket locket
lombong mine
lompat, melompat jump
loncat hop; jump on one foot
longgar loose (wobbly)
lori truck
lorong corridor; lane; alley
limau lemon (citrus)
loteri lottery
luar outside
luar negeri overseas; abroad

luas broad; spacious
lubang hole
lubang hidung nostril
lucah dirty; obscene
lucu funny; cute (appealing)
lucut slip off (dress or shoe); denude
ludah spit
luka injury; injured; wound
luka bakar burn (injury)
lukis, melukis paint
lukisan painting
lulus pass (an exam)
lumayan very profitable
lumba race
lumpuh paralyze
lumpur, berlumpur mud, muddy
lupa forget, forgotten
lupakan, melupakan forget about
luruh worn out (clothes)
lurus straight
lusa the day after tomorrow
lutut knee

M

ma'af! sorry!
mabuk drunk
mabuk laut seasick
macam kind; sort; type
macam apa? what kind of?
madu honey
maha great; very
mahal expensive
mahasiswa university student
mahir skilled
mahkamah court
Mahkamah Tinggi High Court
mahu want
main play
mainan toy; game
majalah magazine
majikan employer
majlis council

M

maju advance; go forward; advanced
mak mother; mum
mak cik aunt
makam mausoleum
makan eat
makan angin sightseeing; holiday; vacation
makan malam evening meal; dinner
makan masa time-consuming
makan pagi breakfast
makan tengah hari lunch
makanan food
makanan laut seafood
makanan ringan snack
makanan segera fast food
maklum; memaklum know; to inform
maklumat information
makmal laboratory
makmur prosperous
makna meaning
maksud, bermaksud meaning; intention; to intend
maktab college
malah opposite (on the contrary)
malam night; evening
malam ini tonight
malam tadi last night
malas lazy
malu ashamed; shy; embarrassed
mampu well off; able to afford something
mana where
mancis matches
mandi bathe; take a shower
manfaat advantage
mangga mango
manggis mangosteen
mangkuk bowl
manik beads
manis sweet
manisan dessert
manja pampered

manusia human being
mara advance
marah angry; upset
mari come; let's
marjerin margarine
markah mark
marmah marbles
martabak Indian pancake with meat filling
masa period; time
masa depan the future
masa lapang free time
masak cook
masakan cooking; cuisine
masalah problem
masalah kecil minor (not important); small matter
masam sour
masam manis sweet and sour
masih still
masin salty
masing-masing each and everyone
masjid mosque
masuk come in; enter
masuk campur meddle
masukkan, memasukkan put inside
mata eye
mata-mata policeman
mata air spring (water)
mata wang currency
matahari sun
matahari terbenam sunset
matahari terbit sunrise
matang mature
mati die; dead
mati tenggelam drown
mahu want; shall; will; would
masyarakat community; society
masyhur famous; well-known
mawar rose
mayat corpse
me- (active verb prefix)
medan square; field
media massa mass media

M

megah proud
meja table
meja makan dining table
meja tulis desk
mekanik mechanic
mekap make-up
mel mail
Melayu Malay
mel udara air mail
melakukan sesuatu have done something
melalui by way of; via
melambai wave
melamun daydream
melancung go on a holiday or vacation
melarikan diri run away
Melayu Malay
meletak kereta park (car)
melipat fold
meluat feel disgust for; loathing
memanaskan heat up (food)
memancing fish
memandu steer; drive
memang indeed; of course
memanggang bake
membahagi-bahagikan hand out
membantah argue; repudiate; protest
membekukan freeze
membela defend (with words)
membereskan sort out (deal with)
memberi makan feed
membetulkan correct
membiayai finance someone/something
membicarakan talk about
membosankan dull (boring)
membuat fotokopi to photocopy
membuat video to videotape
membungkuk stoop
memeluk embrace; hold
memohon ask; beg; plead

mempengaruhi affect
memperkenalkan introduce someone
memperkenalkan diri introduce oneself
mempertahankan defend (in war)
menabung deposit; save
menang win
menangani sign
menantu son-in-law; daughter-in-law
menara tower
menarik interesting
menasihati advise someone
menawarkan offer (suggest opinion or service)
mencampur mix
mencegah prevent
menciptakan create; invent
mencuba attempt; try
menderita suffer
mendesak urgent
mendung cloudy
menelefon dial (a telephone); telephone someone
menemani accompany someone
menemukan discover (be first to find)
menitis drip
mengabaikan ignore
mengalami undergo (hardship)
mengambil gamber to photograph
menganggur unemployed
menganjurkan sponsor something
menghantar deliver something
mengapa? what for?; why?
mengarang create a story
mengasuh bring up children
mengeja spell (words)
mengemukakan bring up a topic
mengeringkan dry something

M

mengerti understand
menghadap opposite (facing); to face
menghapus destroy
menghasilkan earn
mengisi borang fill up a form
menguap yawn
mengubah fikiran change one's mind
mengucapkan pronounce; say something
mengucapkan terima kasih say thank you
mengukur measure out
mengumumkan announce
mengunyah chew
menimbangkan weigh out
meninggal pass away
meninggalkan leave behind; desert; abandon
menjadi anggota kelab belong to a club
menjadi lebih baik improve (a situation)
menjadi lebih kurus lose weight
menjalani undergo
menjelaskan explain
menjijikan disgusting; disgust
menolak decline (refuse)
mentah raw; uncooked; rare; unripe
mentega butter; margarine
menteri minister
menterjemahkan translate
mentol lightbulb
menuju head for (toward)
menunda delay (put off)
menung, termenung ponder; think deeply
menumpang get a lift (ride in a car)
menurun decline (get less)
menurut according to
menyakiti hurt; inflict pain
menyakitkan hati offend; insult

menyapu wipe (hands, face)
menyeberang cross (a road)
menyejukkan cool
menyelamatkan rescue
menyenangkan enjoyable; pleasant
menyerahkan hand over
menyerang attack
menyinggung perasaan offend; insult
menyusahkan troublesome
merah red
merah muda pink
merana languish
merasa bersalah to feel guilty
mercun firecrackers
merdeka freedom
merdu melodious
mereka they; them
meriah happy; joyful
meriam cannon
merosakkan damage; break
merpati pigeon
mesej message
mesin machine
mesin kira adding machine
mesin jawab answering machine
mesin-mesin machinery
meskipun though; although
mesra affectionate; close
mesti necessary; must
mesyuarat meeting
mewah lavish; expensive; luxurious
mi noodles
mihun rice vermicelli
milik, memiliki own; possess
milik dia his; hers
milik orang belong to someone
milik peribadi own (personal)
mimpi a dream; to dream
minat interest
minit minute
minggu week

M

minggu depan next week
minggu yang lalu last week
minta ask for; request
minta maaf apologize;
  say sorry
minum to drink
minuman a drink
minyak oil; fat
minyak bijan sesame oil
minyak masak cooking oil
minyak pelincir grease
minyak rambut hair oil
minyak sapi ghee
minyak tanah kerosene
minyak wangi perfume
minyak zaitun olive oil
mirip alike; similar; look like;
  resemble
misai moustache
misalnya such as (for example)
miskin poor
mitos myth
modal capital (funds)
moden modern
mogok go on strike
mohon request
molek pretty
monorel monorail
montel plump
monyet monkey
motobot motorboat
motokar car
motosikal motorcycle
muat load; carry; fit inside
mubaligh missionary
muda young; unripe
mudah easy
mudah-mudahan hopefully
muka face; across
muka pintu doorway
muka surat page
muka tebal thick-skinned
mula start; begin
mula-mula at first
mulia noble
mulut mouth
mulut murai chatterbox

munasabah reasonable
muncul appear; emerge
muncung muzzle; snout
mundur backward
mungkin maybe; perhaps;
  possibly
muntah vomit
murah cheap; inexpensive;
  good value
murah hati generous
muram somber; sad; dismal
murid pupil; schoolchild
murni pure; clean
musim season
musim bunga spring
musim gugur autumn
musim panas summer
musim sejuk winter
mustahak important
mustahil impossible; incredible
musuh enemy
mutiara pearl
mutu quality
muzik music
muzium museum
Myanmar Burma

N

nabi prophet
nada tone
nadi pulse
nafas breath
nafas baru breathe new life
  (into a project)
nafi deny
nafkah livelihood; alimony
nafsu desire
nahas misfortune
naga dragon
naib deputy
naib johan runner-up
naik go up; climb; rise;
  increase; board (transport);
  ride
naik angin be in bad mood

O

naik darah get into a temper
naik kereta api by rail
naik pangkat get promoted
nakal naughty
nama name
nama keluarga surname;
  family name
nama timang-timangan
  nickname
nampak see; be visible
nampaknya apparently
namun nevertheless
nanas pineapple
nangka jackfruit
nanti later
narkotik narcotics
nasi rice (cooked)
nasi ayam chicken rice
nasi lemak rice cooked in
  coconut milk and served with
  sambal, etc.
nasib fate
nasib baik good luck
nasib tak baik, nasib malang
  unlucky; misfortune
nasihat, menasihati advice;
  to advise
naskah copy; manuscript
negara country; nation
negara dunia ketiga third
  world country
negara maju developed
  country
negara membangun
  developing country
negeri state (of a country)
Negara Thai Thailand
nekad determined
nelayan fisherman
nenek grandmother
nenek moyang ancestor
neraka hell
nganga open mouthed
ngantuk sleepy
ngeri eerie
niaga trade; do business
niat intention

niat baik good intention
niat jahat bad intention
nikah, menikah married; get
  married
nikmati, menikmati enjoy
nilai value
nilon nylon
nombor number
nombor ganjil odd number
nombor genap even number
nombor telefon telephone
  number
nipis thin
nota note
notis notice
novel novel (book)
nyala, bernyala lit
nyaman comfortable; pleasant
nyamuk mosquito
nyanyi, bernyanyi sing
nyanyuk senile
nyaris almost; nearly
nyawa life
nyenyak sound asleep
Nyonya Straits-born Chinese
  lady
nyunyut suck

O

objek object
okay okay
olahraga athletics
olahragawan athlete
oleh by
oleh kerana itu, oleh demikian
  therefore
ombak wave; surf
orang person; human being
orang asing stranger;
  outsider; foreigner
orang atasan upper class
orang awam civilian; the
  public
orang bandar town-dweller
orang barat Westerner

orang Cina Chinese
orang Inggeris British; English
orang Jepun Japanese
orang Jerman German
orang kampung villager
orang Kemboja Cambodian
orang luar stranger; outsider
orang muda young man/woman
orang putih white (English) man
orang ramai the public
orang rumah wife
orang tengah middleman
orang timur Asian; Oriental
orang Tionghua Chinese
orang tua parents; old people
oren orange
otak brain; mind
otot muscle

P

pacat leech
pada on
pada keseluruhannya on the whole
pada masa sekarang nowadays
pada umumnya usually; in general; on the whole
pada waktu malam at night
pada zaman dulu in olden times
padam to go out (fire, candle)
padan matched; fitting well
padang field; square
padang pasir desert
padang rumput grassland
padat solid; dense
paderi priest
padi rice plant
padu united
pagar fence
pagi morning

pagi-pagi early in the morning
paha thigh
pahit bitter
pajak lease; contract
pak father
pak cik uncle
pakai, memakai use; wear
pakaian clothing; garment
pakaian dalam underwear
pakaian seragam uniform
pakar expert
pakar runding consultant
pakat agree
pakatan pact; conspiracy
paket packet
paksa, memaksa forced; compulsion
paku nail
palang crossbar
paling the most
paling dasyat worst
paling kecil smallest
paling penting main (most important)
paling sedikit least
paling utama main (most important)
paling-paling at the most
palsu artificial; counterfeit
pam pump
pamer display; show
pameran a display
panas hot (temperature)
panas terik blistering hot
pancar broadcast; radiate
pancaragam band of musicians
pancut gush out
pandai smart; skillful
pandang view; look at
pandangan panorama; opinion
pandu guide; drive
panduan guidance
panggang, memanggang roasted, roast
panggil, memanggil call; summon

panggilan telefon telephone call

panggilan telefon jarak jauh long-distance telephone call

panggung wayang movie theater

pangkal beginning; base

pangkat rank; station in life

pangkuan lap

pangsapuri apartment

panjang long; length

panjangkan, memanjangkan to extend

panjat, memanjat climb

pantai beach

pantang prohibition

pantas quick; fast

papa poor

papan plank

papan catur chessboard

papan hitam blackboard

papan iklan billboard

papan kenyataan notice board

papaya pawpaw

parah bad; serious (of injury)

parang chopping knife

paras face; level

parfum perfume

parit ditch; drain

parlimen parliament

parti party (political)

paru-paru lungs

pasang, memasang assemble; switch on

pasar market

pasarkan, memasarkan market a product or service

pasar borong wholesale market

pasar malam night market

pasar raya department store; supermarket

pasaran saham share market

pasaran wang money market

pasir sand

pasport passport

pasti sure; certain; definite

pasu pot

pasukan team; military unit

patah broken (of long object)

patah hati broken-hearted

pati essence

patuh obedient

patung statue; doll

payah difficult

payung umbrella

pecah, memecahkan break; shatter

pecat dismiss

pedagang trader

pedang sword

pedas hot (spicy)

pedih sorrowful; painful

peduli bother about; mind

pegang, memegang hold; grasp

pegawai officer

pegawai daerah district officer

pegawai kerajaan government officer

peguam lawyer

peguambela advocate; barrister

peguamcara solicitor

pejabat office

pejabat pos post office

pejam close (eyes)

pekak deaf

pekan small town

pekat thick (of liquids)

pekerjaan job; occupation; profession

pekik scream; yell; shriek

pelabuhan harbor; port

pelacur prostitute

pelampung float; buoy

pelan-pelan slow

pelancung tourist

pelanduk mousedeer

pelanggan customer

pelangi rainbow

pelawa, mempelawa invite

pelayan waiter; waitress

P

pelayan kedai sales assistant; sales clerk
pelekat gum
pelihara take care of; rear
pelik strange; curious
pelita lamp
peluang chance; opportunity
peluh, berpeluh sweat
peluk, berpeluk hug; embrace
pemandangan panoramic view; scenery
pemandu kereta driver
pembantu rumah servant; domestic helper
pemergian departure
pemerintah ruler
pemetik api lighter
pemilik kedai shopkeeper; store owner
pemimpin leader
pen pen
pen mata bulat ballpoint pen
penapis filter
penat tired; weary
pencen retired
pencucuk skewer
pencuri thief
pendapat opinion
pendek short
penderitaan suffering
penduduk inhabitant; resident
penelitian research
penerbangan flight (plane)
pengalaman, mengalami an experience; experience
pengambilan barang hilang lost property
pengantin lelaki bridegroom
pengantin perempuan bride
penganut Buddha Buddhist
penganut Islam Muslim
penganut Kristian Christian
pengarah director
pengarang editor
pengaruh, mempengaruhi influence; affect

pengebumian funeral
pengeluaran output; production
pengesahan confirmation
penggal term; paragraph
penggal sekolah school term
penggembara traveler
penghulu village headman
penghuni inhabitant; resident; tenant
pengsan fainted
pengumuman notice; announcement
pengurangan reduction
pengurus manager
peniaga businessperson
pening dizzy
peninggalan omission
penis penis
penjara jail; prison
penjara seumur hidup life imprisonment
penjelasan clarification
penjuru corner; angle
penolakan refusal
pensel pencil
pensyarah lecturer
penterjemah translator; interpreter
penting important; major
penuh full
penuh harapan full of hope
penuh sesak congested
penuhi, memenuhi to fulfill
penulis writer
penumpang passenger
penurunan reduction
penutup lid
penyakit disease; illness
penyapu broom
penyeluk saku pickpocket
penyepit chopsticks
penyek flattened
penyu turtle
peperiksaan examination
perabot furniture
perah squeeze; wring

P

perahu boat
perajurit soldier
perak silver
peranan role
perang war; battle
perangai behavior
perasaan emotion
peraturan rule; regulation
peratus per cent
perayaan festival; celebration
perbaiki, memperbaiki mend
perbatasan border (between countries); limit
perbelanjaan expense
perbezaan difference
perbezaan pendapat to have different opinions
percakapan conversation
percaya trust; believe; have confidence in
percubaan attempt
perdagangan trade
perdana menteri prime minister
perempuan woman; female
pergelangan tangan wrist
pergi go; leave
perhatikan, memperhatikan notice; pay attention to
perhentian bas bus stop
peribadi private
perigi well (water)
periksa, memeriksa examine; inspect
perintah a command
peristiwa event; incident
periuk pan
perjalanan journey; trip
perjanjian agreement
perkahwinan wedding
perkakas tools
perkara matter
perkembangan development
perlahan slow
perlu need
permaidani carpet; mat; rug
permit permit (license)

permukaan surface
permulaan start (beginning)
pernah have already
perniagaan business
pernikahan wedding
perpustakaan library
persetujuan agreement
pertama first
pertandingan match (game)
pertanyaan question
pertunjukan show; performance
perubatan medical
perusahaan business
perut stomach; belly; abdomen
pesan, memesan to order
pesawat airplane
pesta party; festival; celebration
pesuruhjaya commissioner
peta map
peta bumi world map
petang late afternoon; evening
petang ini this evening
petang esok tomorrow evening
peti crate
peti sejuk refrigerator
petik pluck
petir thunder
petrol petrol; fuel; gas
petunjuk sign
piala cup
picit squeeze; press; massage
pihak party; side
pihak berkuasa the authorities
pijak, memijak step on
pijama pyjamas
pil pills
pilih, memilih choose; select
pilihan choice
pindah, memindah move
pinggir sungai bank of river
pinjam, meminjam borrow
pinjami, meminjami lend
pintar smart

P

pintu door
pintu gerbang gate
pintu keluar exit (way out)
pintu masuk entrance (way in)
pipi cheek
piring plate; dish
pisah, memisahkan separate
pisang banana
pisau knife
pita ribbon; tape
pita pelekat adhesive tape
plag plug
plaster adhesive tape; sticking plaster
plastik plastic
pohon tree; bush
poket pocket
polis police
polisi policy
politik politics
pondok hut; shack
popular popular
pos berdaftar registered mail
pos biasa surface mail
pos udara air mail
poskad postcard
potong, memotong slice; cut; break (rope, cable)
potongan harga discount
presiden president
Puan Mrs; Madam
puas satisfied
puasa, berpuasa fasting
puaskan, memuaskan satisfy
pujian, memuji praise
pukul, memukul o'clock; strike
pukul berapa? what time?
pula again; also; yet
pulang go back
pulau island
pulih recover
puluh ten; multiples of ten
puncak peak; summit
punggung back (part of body)
punya, mempunyai have; own; possess

pura-pura, berpura-pura pretend
purata on average
purba ancient
pusat center
pusat bandar center of city
pusing dazed; dizzy; ill
putar, berputar to turn around
putera prince
puteri princess
putih white
putus break off
putus asa give up hope
putuskan, memutuskan decide

R

raba grope
Rabu Wednesday
rabun poor sight
racun poison
radang, meradang angry, to be angry
raga basket; wicker ball
ragam way; manner; act up
ragu-ragu be doubtful
rahang jaw
rahim uterus; womb
rahmat blessing
rahsia secret
rai, meraikan entertain; celebrate; receive as guest
raja king
rajah diagram
rajin hardworking; industrious
rajuk, merajuk sulk; sulky
rak shelf
rakaman recording
rakan colleague; friend
rakan kongsi business partner
rakit raft
rakyat people
Ramadan Muslim fasting month

ramah friendly; open
ramai many; a large number
rama-rama butterfly
ramalan prediction
ramalan cuaca weather forecast
rambut hair
rancang, merancang plan
rancangan a plan
rangkak crawl
rangup crisp
rantai chain
rantai leher necklace
rantai tangan bracelet
rapat be close together
rapi, merapikan orderly; make orderly; make neat; tidy
rasa, merasa feel; taste
rasa sakit feel ill
rasmi official
rasmikan, merasmikan open officially; inaugurate
rasuah bribe
rata even; level
ratu queen
ratus hundred
rawat, merawat take care of; treat (medically)
rayakan, merayakan celebrate (a holiday)
reben ribbon
rebus boiled
rebut fight about; fight over
regu team
rehat rest
remaja youth; teenager
rempah-rempah spices
renang, berenang swim
rencana article
rendah low
rendam, merendam soak
resepi recipe
resit receipt
restoran restaurant
retak crack; cracked
ribu thousand
rindu to miss (a loved one)

ringan light (not heavy); mild
ringkas concise
roda wheel
rokok, merokok cigarette; smoke
rombongan group
rosak broken
roti bread
ruang room; space
ruang bawah downstairs
rugi lose money
rugikan, merugikan cause to lose money
rukun pillar; principle; foundation
rumah house; home
rumah persinggahan lodge; small hotel; rest house
rumah tumpangan guesthouse
rumit complicated
rumput grass
rupa appearance
rupanya apparently
rupa-rupanya seem to be
rusa deer

S

saat moment; instant
sabar patient
Sabtu Saturday
sabun soap
sabun cuci baju detergent (for clothes)
sabun cuci piring detergent (for eating utensils)
sabut husk (of coconut)
sagu sago
sah legal
sahabat friend
saham share (of company)
saing, bersaing compete
saingan competition
saja only

sajak poem
sajian dish; food
sakit sick; ill; sore (painful); ache
sakit hati annoyed
sakit jiwa mentally ill; insane
sakit kepala headache
sakit perut stomachache
saksama just; impartial
saksi witness
sakti sacred power; have mystical or religious power
saku pocket
salah wrong; false; mistaken
salah anggap misjudge
salah faham misunderstanding
salah guna misuse; abuse
salah jalan took the wrong road or turning
salah satu either
salahkan, menyalahkan fault
salam greetings
salin change (clothes)
salinan copy
saling mutually
salji snow
salur lead into
salur darah blood vessel
salur nadi artery
saluran channel
sama the same; identical
sama-sama you're welcome
saman summons
sambal chili sauce
sambil while
sambilan part-time
sambung, menyambung connect
sambungan connection (telephone)
sambut, menyambut receive; welcome (visitor)
sami Buddhist or Hindu priest
sampah garbage
sampai arrive; reach; until
sampai berjumpa lagi goodbye; see you later

sampan native boat
samping side
sampul wrapping; cover
sampul surat envelope
sana there (out of sight)
sanak saudara relatives
sanar lean against
sandiwara stage play
sangat quite; really (very); extremely; such (quantity)
sanggul hair bun; knot of hair
sanggup be capable of; be willing to take on
sangka, menyangka suspicion; suspect
sangkut hang on a hook
santai, bersantai relax
santan coconut milk
santapan cuisine (style of cooking)
sapi beef; cow
sapu broom
sapu tangan handkerchief
sara hidup livelihood
sarang nest
sarapan pagi breakfast
sarkas circus
sarung sarong; wrap-around skirt
sarung bantal pillowcase
sarung kaki socks
sastera literature
satay barbecued meat on skewers
satu one
satu-satunya single (only one)
saudara relatives; you (unfamiliar, formal, polite)
sawah rice padi
sawi putih Chinese cabbage
saya I; me
sayang be fond of; have affection for someone; unfortunately
sayanglah! what a shame!
sayap wing
sayur, sayuran vegetables

S

sayuran hijau greens
se- (prefix meaning 'one' or 'the same as')
sebab because
sebahagian partly; portion of
sebahagian besar mainly; majority; large part
sebaliknya instead; on the contrary; opposite
sebelah next to
sebelas eleven
sebelum before
sebelumnya used to do something; first; beforehand
sebentar in a moment; brief period
seberang across from
sebut, menyebut say
secara by means of; by way of
sedang be in the middle of
sedap delicious
sedar, menyedari realize; be conscious
sederhana modest; simple; plain
sedia available
sediakan, menyediakan prepare; make ready
sedih sad; unhappy; upset
sedikit little; few; not much; slight
sedikit demi sedikit gradually; little by little
segala every
segala-galanya everything
segar fresh
segera soon
segi angle; side
segi tiga triangle
segi empat rectangle
seharusnya ought to
sehat healthy
sehelai a piece (of paper)
seimbang equal
sejak since
sejarah history

sejuk cool
sekali once; one time
sekalian at the same time; at once
sekarang now; at present
sekarang juga immediately; right now
sekolah school
seks sex (sexual activity)
sekurang-kurangnya at least
selain apart from
selalu always
selama ini all this while
selamanya forever
selamat safe; to survive (an accident)
selamat jalan bon voyage; goodbye
selamat datang welcome
selamat pagi good morning
selamat malam goodnight
selamat tahun baru happy new year!
selamat tengah hari good afternoon
selamat tinggal (to those leaving behind) goodbye
selamat ulang tahun happy birthday!
Selasa Tuesday
selat straits
selatan south
selendang shawl
selenggarakan, menyelenggarakan organize; hold (an event)
selesai finish; end; cease
selewat-lewatnya at the latest
selidiki, menyelidiki study; research
selimut blanket
selipar sandals
selisih difference
selisih faham misunderstanding
selsema cold; influenza

S

seluar dalam panties; briefs; underpants

seluar panjang long pants; trousers

seluar pendek short pants

seludup smuggle

seluruh entire; whole

semak, menyemak check to improve

semalam last night; yesterday

semangat spirit

semasa during

sembahkan, persembahkan present

sembahyang pray; worship

sembilan nine

sembilan belas nineteen

sembilan puluh ninety

sembuh cured; recovered

sembunyi hide

sembur, menyembur spray

sementara temporarily

sementara itu meanwhile

sempat have an opportunity to

sempit narrow

sempurna complete

semua all

semua orang everybody; everyone

senang easy

sendiri self; oneself; alone

sendirian by oneself; all alone; on one's own

senduk ladle

seni art

seniman artist

senja dusk

senjata weapon

sentuh, menyentuh touch

senyum, tersenyum smile

sepatu shoes

seperempat one-quarter

seperti like; as

sepertiga one-third

seperti itu such (like that)

sepi quiet; still

sepuluh ten

sepuluh ribu ten thousand

serai lemongrass

serangga insect

seratus one hundred

seratus ribu one hundred thousand

serba all sorts

sering often; common (frequent)

serta, beserta with

seruling flute

serupa identical

servis service

sesat lost

seseorang somebody; someone

sesuai dengan adapted; suited

sesuaikan, menyesuaikan adapt to

sesuatu something

sesuatu tempat somewhere

sesudah after

stesen kereta api train station

stesen minyak gas station; petrol station

set set (a set of cups)

setelah after

setem stamp (for letter)

setengah half

setia loyal

setiap hari daily

setiausaha secretary

seumur hidup lifetime

sewa, menyewa rent; hire

sewakan, menyewakan rent out

sia-sia to no avail

siang daytime

siap, bersiap ready

siapa? who?

siapa saja anybody; anyone

siapkan make ready

siapkan meja makan lay the table

siaran, menyiarkan broadcast

sibuk busy (doing something)

sifat characteristic
sijil certificate
sikap attitude
sikat, menyikat brush
silakan please
siling ceiling
simpan, menyimpan keep; store
simpang, menyimpang diverge from
simpangan intersection
sinar rays
singkat concise; short
sini here
sisa leftovers; remainder
sisi side; flank
sisir comb
sistem system
siswazah university graduate
situ over there (within sight)
skirt skirt
skrin komputer computer screen
soal, soalan ask; question
soket socket (electric)
songkok Malay headwear
sopan polite; well-mannered
sos ikan fish sauce
soto spiced soup
sotong squid
span sponge
spring spring (of bed)
stor store (place to keep things)
suami husband
suara voice
suasana atmosphere
suatu one
subuh dawn
subur fertile
suci holy
sudah already
sudah bangun awake
sudah biasa used to (accustomed)
sudah naik on board (train, boat, bus)

sudu spoon
sudut corner
suhu temperature
suis switch (light switch)
suka, menyukai to like
sukar difficult
sukar didapat difficult to get
suku tribe; people
sulaman embroidery
sulit difficult
sungai river
sungguh really; truly
suntik inject; vaccinate
sunyi quiet; still
sup soup
supaya in order that; so that
surat letter; mail
surat khabar newspaper
surat-menyurat correspond (write letters)
suruh, menyuruh instruct; command
susah difficult
susu milk
susul, menyusul follow up
sut suit (of clothes)
sutera silk
swasta private (business)
syak suspect
syampu shampoo
syarahan lecture
syarat pre-condition; indication
syariah Islamic law
syarikat company
syok appealing; fun
syukur thankful

T

tabiat behavior
tadi a while ago; earlier (within the day)
tadika kindergarten
tafsir, menafsir estimate; interpret
tagih, menaglh crave for

tahan hold back; restrain; endure
tahan lasak hardy
tahanan detention
tahap level; standard
tahi dung; excrement
tahniah congratulations
tahu know; soybean curd (tofu)
tahun year; years
tahun depan next year
tahun lepas last year
taip, menaip type
taja, menaja sponsor
tajam sharp
tajuk (of writing) title
tak no; not
tak ada don't have
takut fear; frightened; scared
takziah condolence
talam tray
tali rope; string
tali leher necktie
tali pinggang belt
talian line (of a telephone)
tamak greedy
taman garden; park
taman bunga botanic gardens
tamat ended
tambah add; increase; plus
tambahan extra (additional)
tambahan lagi in addition
tampal, menampal stick
tambang fare
tambang pergi-balik two-way fare
tampan handsome
tamu guest; visitor
tanah land; ground (earth)
tanah milik property
tanam, menanam plant
tanaman plant; crop
tanda sign; indication
tandas toilet; restroom
tandatangan signature
tandus barren (land)
tangan hand; forearm

tangga stairs; ladder
tanggapan impression
tanggung guaranteed
tanggungjawab be responsible
tangis, menangis cry
tangkai handle
tangkap, menangkap grasp; capture; catch
tangki air water tank
tanpa without
tanya, bertanya ask; enquire
tari, menari dance
tarian a dance
tarif tariff
tarik pull
tarikh lahir date of birth
taring tusk (of an animal)
taruh, menaruh place; bet
tasik lake
tatatertib rules of behavior
taufan typhoon
taun cholera
tawar having no flavor
tawar hati disheartened
tawar menawar bargain
tawaran offer
tayangan wayang film show
tayar tire
teater theater
tebal (of things) thick
tebang, menebang cut down
tebu sugarcane
tebuk perforate; punch a hole (in a piece of paper)
teduh shade; shelter
tegang tense
tegas firm; strict
tegur warn
teguran warning
teh tea
teka guess
teka-teki riddle
tekak throat
tekan press
tekanan pressure; stress

T

teksi taxi
telaga pond
telanjang naked
telefon telephone
telefon bimbit cell phone; mobile phone
telekung praying veil of Muslim women (usually white in color)
televisyen television; TV
telinga ear
teliti meticulous; thorough
teluk bay
telur egg
telur dadar omelette
telur masin salted egg
teman friend
teman lelaki boyfriend
teman perempuan girlfriend
tembaga copper
tembak, menembak shoot
tembakau tobacco
tembikai watermelon
tembikar pottery; chinaware
tembok wall
tembus, menembus pierce; penetrate
tempah, menempah reserve, make reservation
tempat place; location
tempat mandi shower; bathroom
tempat tidur bedroom
tempatan local
tempayan large earthenware
tempeh fermented soybean cake
tempoh duration; period
tempur, menempur collide
tempuran collision
tempurung coconut shell
temu, bertemu, menemui meet
temuduga interview
temujanji appointment
tenaga power
tenang calm; peaceful
tendang kick

tengah middle; center
tengah hari midday
tengah malam midnight
tenggara southeast
tenggelam submerged; drowned
tengkar, bertengkar argue
tengkolok cloth headgear of Malay man
tengkorak skull
tengkuk neck
tengok, menengok see; visit
tentang concerning
tentangan; bertentang challenge; objection; at odds
tentera armed forces
tentera darat land army
tentera laut navy
tentera udara air force
tentu certain; certainly
tentukan, menentukan fix a time; establish
tenun, menenun weave
tenunan weaving
tenung stare
tepat exact; exactly
tepat pada waktu punctual; on time
tepi edge; fringe; side
tepi sungai river bank
tepuk tangan clap hands
tepung flour
tepung beras rice flour
tepung gandum wheat flour
tepung jagung corn flour
tepung susu milk powder
terakhir last; final
terang light; clear; bright
terang-terang openly; frankly
terbakar on fire
terbang, menerbang fly
terbit, menerbitkan publish
tercatat noted
terdahulu past; former
tergantung it depends; to depend on

terhadap as regards; regarding; towards

teriak shout

terima, menerima receive; accept

terima kasih thank you

terjadi happened

terjemah translate

terjun fall; jump; leap

terkejut surprised

terkenal famous

terlalu too (excessive)

terlambat late

terletak located; situated

terminal terminal

ternakan livestock

terompah wooden clogs

teropong telescope

terowong tunnel

terperangkap stuck (won't move); trapped

terpisah separate

tersembunyi hidden

tersesat lost (can't find way)

tersinggung upset; unhappy; insulted

tertarik pada interested in

tertawa laugh

teruk very bad

terung eggplant; aubergine

terus straight ahead; non-stop

teruskan, meneruskan continue

testikel testicles

tetamu guest

tetangga neighbor

tetap fixed; permanent

tetapi but

tetek breasts

tiada not any

tiada siapapun nobody

tiang post; column

tiap every

tiba arrive

tiba-tiba suddenly

tidak no; not

tidak ada absent

tidak apa never mind

tidak apa-apa nothing

tidak boleh cannot

tidak cukup lacking; not enough

tidak hadir absent

tidak jelas vague; unclear

tidak ada masalah it doesn't matter; no problem

tidak mungkin impossible

tidak nakal not naughty; well-behaved

tidak pedas mild (not hot or spicy)

tidak sah illegal

tidak sopan impolite; rude

tidak suka dislike

tidak terlambat on time; not late

tidak usah not necessary

tidak wajib optional

tidur sleep; go to bed

tidur mati sleep like a log

tiga three

tiga belas thirteen

tiga puluh thirty

tikam, menikam stab

tikar mat

tiket ticket

tiket pergi-balik return ticket

tiket untuk satu arah sahaja one-way ticket

tikus mouse; rat

tilam mattress

timah tin

timba bucket

timbang weigh; contemplate

timbangan scales (for weighing)

timbangkan, pertimbangkan consider

timbul, menimbul appear; emerge from

timbun heap; pile; stack

timun cucumber

timur east

timur laut northeast

tin tin
tindak, bertindak act
tindakan action
tinggal depart; live; reside; stay
tinggalkan leave behind; depart
tinggi tall; high
tingkap window
tingkat level; story of a building
tingkatan form (class in secondary school)
tinjau, meninjau survoy
tipis (of liquids) shallow
tip tip (for services)
tipu, menipu deceive; cheat
tiram oysters
tiruan imitation; artificial
tisu tissue
titi wooden bridge
titik drop
titik berat, menitikberatkan give importance to; emphasize
tiup, bertiup blow
tocang braid; plait
tokoh important figure or personality
tokong Hindu or Buddhist temple
tolak, menolak refuse; object (protest)
tolak ansur give and take
tolong, menolong help; assist
tomato tomato
tong barrel
tonjol, menonjol stick out
tonton, menonton watch; observe
topeng mask
topi hat
tradisi tradition
trengkas shorthand
tua old (of persons); dark color
tuak palm wine
tuala towel
tuala mandi bath towel

tuala wanita sanitary towel
tuan sir; owner; master
tuan rumah house owner
tuang, menuang pour
tubuh body
tuduh, menuduh accuse
tudung head covering of Muslim women; lid; cover
tugas job; duties
tugu monument
Tuhan God
tuju, menuju towards
tujuan destination; goal
tujuh seven
tujuh belas seventeen
tujuh puluh seventy
tukang tradesperson; craftsperson
tukang gaji servant
tukang gunting rambut barber
tukang masak cook
tukar, menukar exchange
tulang bone
tulang belakang spine
tuli deaf
tulis, menulis write
tulisan written work
tumbuh, bertumbuh grow (larger, up)
tumbuhan growth
tumbuk pound
tunai cash
tunang lelaki fiancé
tunang perempuan fiancée
tunda, ditunda postpone; postponed
tunggal single; sole
tunggu, menunggu wait; wait for
tunjuk point out; guide
tuntut, menuntut demand
turun go down; get off (transport)
turut obey; obedient
turut-menurut in sequence
tutup, menutup close; cover

U

U

ubah, berubah change
ubahsuai modify
uban gray hair
ubat medicine
ubat angin ointment
ubat gigi toothpaste
ubi tapioca
ubin tile
ucap, berucap express; say
ucapan speech
udang shrimp; prawn
udang galah lobster
udang kering dried shrimp
udara air
uji test; try out
uji bakat audition
ujian test
ujikaji experiment
ukir, mengukir carve; sculpt; engrave
ukiran carving; sculpture; engraving
ukur, mengukur measure
ukuran measurement; size
ulam raw vegetables eaten with rice
ulama Muslim scholar
ulang, mengulangi repeat
ulang kaji revision
ulang tahun anniversary
ulang-alik to-and-fro
ular snake
ulat worm
umat follower
umpama example
umpamanya such as (for example)
umum general; public
umumnya generally; mostly
umur age
umur panjang longevity
umurnya berapa? how old is he/she?
undang, mengundang invite
undang-undang laws

undangan invitation
undi vote
undur reverse; back up
unggu purple
unggul excellent
unta camel
untuk for; in place of
untuk apa? what for?
untuk dijual for sale
untung profit
upacara ceremony
upah fee
upaya means; abilty; effort
urat sinew; tendon; vein
urus arrange; manage
urusan affair; matter
urusniaga business deal
urut; mengurut massage
usah don't
usaha effort; activity; one's best
usaha sama joint venture
usahawan entrepreneur
usia age
usik, mengusik tease
usir, mengusir chase away; chase out
usul origin
utama most important; chief; major
utara north
uzur very weak; very sick

W

wabak outbreak of disease; epidemic
wad ward (of hospital)
waja steel
wajah feature of the face
wajar appropriate
wajib compulsory; necessary; obligatory
wakil agent; representative
wakil rakyat people's representative in parliament

waktu when; time
waktu lapang free time
waktu makan mealtime
waktu tidur bedtime
walaupun although; though; even if
walhal in fact
walhasil in the end; eventually
wali guardian
wang money
wang baki change
wang belanja pocket money
wang kertas currency note
wang tunai cash
wangi sweet-smelling; fragrant
wanita lady; woman; female
wap steam; vapor
warak devout; religious; pious
waras sane
warganegara citizen of a country
waris heir; inheritor
warisan heritage
warna color
warna-warni colorful
warta berita news
warta kerajaan government gazette
wartawan journalist; reporter
warung stall; eating stall
wasiat will
was-was hesitate; doubt
wat Buddhist temple
watak character; personality
wau kite (from state of Kelantan)
wawancara interview
wawasan vision
wayang gambar movie
wayang kulit shadow puppet play

wayar wire
wilayah province; region
wira hero
wisma building
wujud exist

Y

ya yes
yakin believe; confident
yang the one who; that which
yang banyak lots of
Yang Berhormat The Honorable (when addressing a government minister or member of parliament)
yang lain something else
yang mana? which?
yatim orphan
yayasan foundation (non-profit organization)
yuran fee; subscription

Z

zaitun olive
zakar penis
zakat tithe
zalim cruel; wicked
zaman epoch; particular period; era
zaman gemilang golden age
zaman sekarang the present day
zat nutrient
ziarah, berziarah to visit
zina adultery
zoo zoo
zukini courgette (zucchini)

English–
Bahasa Malaysia

A

abdomen perut
able to boleh
about (approximately) kira-kira; lebih kurang
about (regarding) tentang; mengenai
above (upstairs) di atas
abroad luar negera
abruptly tiba-tiba
absent tidak hadir; tidak ada
absorb serap, menyerap
absurd mustahil
abuse salahguna
accept, to terima, menerima
acceptable boleh diterima
access jalan masuk
accident kemalangan
accidentally (by chance) tidak sengaja
accommodation penginapan
accompany, to ikut; menemani
accomplish mencapai
according to menurut; mengikut
accordingly sewajarnya
account kira-kira; akaun
accountant akauntan
accurate tepat
accuse, to tuduh, menuduh
ache sakit
achieve mencapai
achievement pencapaian
acquaintance kenalan
across from seberang
act, to tindak, bertindak

action tindakan; pergerakan
active cergas; rancak
activity kegiatan; activiti
actual betul; benar
actually kebetulan; sebenarnya
adapt menyesuaikan
add, to tambah, menambah
additional tambahan
address alamat; ucapan
adequate memadai; mencukupi
adhesive pelekat
adjust membetulkan
administration pentadbiran; pengurusan
admit (confess) akui
adolescent remaja
adult dewasa
advance (go forward) maju
advance (money, a deposit) wang pendahuluan
advantage faedah; kebaikan
advice nasihat
advocate peguambela
aeroplane pesawat; kapal terbang
affair perkara; urusan
affect, to pengaruh, mempengaruhi
affection sayang
afford, to (buy something) mampu
afraid takut; ngeri
after sesudah; setelah
afternoon tengah hari
afternoon (3 pm to dusk) petang

A

ENGLISH—BAHASA MALAYSIA

afterwards (then) kemudian
again sekali lagi; semula
against menentang
age umur
agent wakil; ejen
ago (in the past) dulu
agree, to setuju, menyetujui
agreement perjanjian;
  persetujuan
air udara
air conditioner alat hawa
  dingin
air force tentera udara
air mail pos udara; mel udara
airport lapangan terbang
alcohol (liquor) alkohol; arak
alike mirip
alive hidup
all semua; seluruh; segala
alley (lane) lorong
allowed to boleh
almost hampir
alone sendiri; sendirian
alphabet abjad
already sudah
also juga; pun
altogether (in total) berjumlah
although walaupun
always selalu; sentiasa
ambassador duta besar
America Amerika Syarikat
American orang Amerika
among antara; di antara
amount jumlah
ancestor nenek moyang
ancient lama
and dan
angry marah
animal binatang
ankle gelang kaki
annoyed menyakitkan hati
another (different) yang lain
another (same again) satu lagi
answer (in response)
  jawapan; balas
answer (to respond) jawab,
  berjawab, menjawab

answer (to respond in writing)
  balas; membalas
answer the phone jawab
  telefon
antiques barang antik
anus dubur
anybody, anyone siapa saja
anything apa saja
anywhere ke mana saja
apart berpisahan
apart from selain
apartment apartmen
apologize, to minta maaf
apparently rupanya
appear (become visible)
  muncul; timbul
appearance (looks) rupa
appliance (electrical) alat letrik
apply, to (for permission)
  memohon izin
appointment temujanji
approach, to (in space)
  mendekati; menghampiri
approach, to (in time)
  menjelang
appropriate sesuai
approximately kira-kira; lebih
  kurang
approval kebenaran
architecture seni bina
area wilayah; daerah; kawasan
argue, to tengkar, bertengkar
arm lengan
armchair kerusi tangan
army tentera darat
armed forces angkatan
  tentera
aroma bau harum
around (approximately)
  kira-kira; lebih kurang
around (nearby) dekat
around (surrounding)
  sekeliling; di sekitar
arrange, to atur; urus
arrangements (planning)
  perancangan
arrive, to tiba; datang

B

art seni
artificial buatan tiruan; palsu
artist seniman
as well (also) juga
ashamed (embarrassed) malu
Asia Asia
ask about, to tanya
ask for (request) minta,
  meminta
assemble (gather) kumpul,
  berkumpul
assemble (put together)
  pasang, memasang
assist, to bantu, membantu
astonished heran
at di
at home di rumah
at night pada waktu malam
at once (at the same time)
  sekali
at once (now) sekarang
at once (together) bersama
at the latest selewat-lewatnya
attain (reach), to capai,
  mencapai
attempt, to mencuba
attend, to hadir
attitude sikap
attractive (man) tampan
attractive (woman) cantik
auction, to lelong, melelong
August Ogos
aunt emak saudara
automobile (car) kereta
author penulis
autumn musim gugur
available sedia, tersedia
avenue lebuh; jalan
average (numbers) purata
average (so-so, just okay)
  sederhana
awake (wake up) bangun,
  membangun
aware sedar
awful dasyat
awhile sebentar; sekejap
ax kapak

baby bayi
bachelor bujang
back (rear) belakang
back, to go kembali
back up, to undur, mengundur
background latar belakang
backward terbalik; mundur
bad buruk; jahat; busuk
bad luck tak bernasik baik
badge lencana; lambang
baggage bagasi
bake, to panggang,
  memanggang; bakar,
  membakar
bald botak
ball bola
ballpoint pen pen mata bulat
banana pisang
band pancaragam
bandage kain pembalut
bank (of river) pinggir; tepi
bank manager pengurus bank
bar (blocking way) halang
bar (serving drinks) bar
barber tukang gunting rambut
barefoot berkaki ayam
barely hampir tidak
bargain, to tawar-menawar
barrier halangan; rintangan
barrister peguambela
basic dasar; asas
basket bakul; raga
basketball bola keranjang
bathe (swim) berenang
bathe (take a bath) mandi
bathroom bilik mandi
bay teluk
be (exist) ada
beach pantai
bead manik
bean kacang
beancurd tahu
beard janggut
beat (to defeat) kalahkan
beat (to strike) pukul

B

beautiful (places) indah
beautiful (things) bagus
beautiful (women) cantik
beauty kecantikan
because kerana; sebab
become, to jadi, menjadi
bed katil
bedroom bilik tidur
bedsheet cadar
beef daging lembu
before (in front of) di depan
before (in time) sebelum;
  terdahulu
beforehand (earlier) sebelum
  itu; terlebih dahulu
beforehand (within the day)
  tadi
begin, to mula, bermula
behavior kelakuan; perangai
behind di belakang
being wujud; ada
belief (faith) kepercayaan;
  keyakinan
believe, to percaya; yakin
bell loceng
belong kepunyaan
below (downstairs) di bawah
belt tali pinggang
bench bangku
bend (in road) selekoh
benefit faedah; manfaat
beside di samping; di sebelah
besides lagi pula; selain; di
  samping
best paling baik; paling bagus
best wishes (to end letter)
  salam sejahtera
bet bertaruh; berjudi
better lebih baik; lebih bagus
better, get (be cured) sembuh
between di antara
beverage minuman
beware berjaga-jaga; awas
beyond seterusnya
bicycle basikal
big (area) luas
big (size) besar

bill bil
billboard papan iklan
billion bilion
bird burung
birth, to give lahir, melahirkan
birthday hari ulang tahun; hari
  jadi
biscuit (salty, cracker) kraker
biscuit (sweet, cookie) biskut
bit (part) bahagian
bit (slightly) sedikit
bite, to gigit, menggigit
bitter pahit
black hitam
blame, to salah, menyalahkan
bland tawar; hambar
blank kosong
blanket selimut; gebar
blind (person) buta
bliss kebahagian
blood darah
blood pressure tekanan darah
blouse blaus
blow tiup
blue biru
blunt tumpul
board, to (bus, train) naik,
  menaik
boat perahu; bot
body badan; tubuh; anggota
boil, to rebus, merebus; jerang
bold berani
bolster bantal peluk
bone tulang
book buku
bookshop kedai buku
booth warung; gerai; pondok
border (between countries)
  sempadan
border (edge) perbatasan;
  pinggiran
bored bosan; jemu
born, to be lahir, dilahir
borrow, to pinjam, meminjam
botanic gardens kebun
  bunga; taman bunga
both dua-duanya; keduanya

bother (disturb), to ganggu, mengganggu
bottle botol
bouquet jambak bunga
bow (head) tunduk
bowl mangkuk
box kotak; peti
boy budak lelaki
boyfriend teman lelaki
bracelet gelang tangan
brain otak
brake (vehicle) brek
branch cabang; dahan; cawangan
brand jenama
brass tembaga
brave (daring) berani
bread roti
break, to (shatter) pecah, memecahkan
break down, to (car, machine) rosak
breakfast (morning meal) makan pagi; sarapan pagi
breasts buah dada; tetek
breath nafas
breeze bayu
breezy berangin
bribe rasuah
bride pengantin perempuan
bridegroom pengantin lelaki
bridge jambatan; titi
brief (time) sebentar
briefcase beg dokumen
briefs seluar dalam
bright terang; bercahaya
bright (color) terang
bright (person) pandai
bring, to bawa, membawa
bring up (children) mengasuh
bring up (topic) mengemukakan
British orang Inggeris
broad (length) lebar
broad (spacious) luas
broadcast (program) siaran
brochure risalah

broken (does not work) rosak
broken (shattered) pecah
broken (snapped) patah
broken off putus
bronze gangsa
brooch kerongsang
broom penyapu
broth (soup) sup
brother abang lelaki
brother (older) abang
brother (younger) adik
brother-in-law abang ipar
brown coklat
brown sugar gula merah
bruise lebam; bengkak
brush sikat; berus
brush, to sikat, menyikat; gosok, menggosok
bucket baldi; timba
Buddhism agama Buddha
Buddhist penganut Buddha
buffalo (water buffalo) kerbau
build, to bangun, membangun; bina, membina
building bangunan
bulb mentol
burn, to bakar, membakar
Burma Myanmar
Burmese orang Myanmar
bus bas
bus station stesen bas
bus stop perhentian bas
bush belukar
business perniagaan; perdagangan
businessperson peniaga; pedagang
busy (crowded) ramai orang
busy (doing something) sibuk
but tetapi
butter mentega
butterfly kupu-kupu; rama-rama
buttock buntut; punggung
button butang
buy, to beli, membeli
bye-bye selamat tinggal

C

cab teksi
cabbage kobis
cabbage (Chinese) sawi
cabinet almari; kabinet
cable kawat; kabel
cake (pastry) kueh
calculate hitung; kira
calculator mesin kira; kalkulator
call, to panggil, memanggil
call on the telephone menelefon
calm tenang; sabar
Cambodia Kemboja
Cambodian orang Kemboja
camera kamera
can (be able to) boleh
can (tin) tin
cancel, to batal, membatal
candle lilin
candy (sweets) gula-gula
cane rotan; buluh
canoe perahu
capable cekap
capital (country) ibu negara
capital (money) modal
capital (state) ibu negeri
capital city ibu kota
captivate memikat hati
capture, to tangkap, menangkap
car (automobile) kereta; motokar
car park tempat letak kereta; medan letak kereta
cardboard kadbod
cards (game) kad
care for (love) sayang; cinta
careful! hati-hati!; awas!
careless leka; lalai; tidak cermat
career kerjaya
carnival pesta; karnival
carpet permaidani
carrot lobak merah

carry, to bawa, membawa
carve, to ukir, mengukir
cash (money) wang tunai
cash a check, to tunaikan cek
cash price harga tunai
cashier juruwang
cassette kaset
cat kucing
catch, to tangkap, menangkap
category kumpulan; golongan; kategori
cauliflower kobis bunga
cause, to sebab, menyebab
causeway tambak
cautious hati-hati
cave gua
ceiling siling
celebration perayaan
celery daun saderi
cell phone telefon bimbit
cemetery tanah perkuburan
center (middle) pusat; tengah
center (of city) pusat kota
central pusat
century abad; kurun
ceremony upacara
certain (sure) pasti; tentu
certainly! memang!
certificate sijil
chain rantai; rangkaian
chair kerusi
chairman pengerusi
chamber bilik
champion juara; jaguh; johan
chance (opportunity) kesempatan; peluang
chance, by kebetulan
change (coins) duit syiling
change, to (conditions, situations) ubah
change, to (exchange money) tukar
change, to (switch clothes) salin; ganti
change one's mind tukar fikiran
channel saluran; selat

c

chaos kacau-bilau; huru-hara
chapel gereja kecil
chapter bab
character (personality) watak
character (written) huruf
characteristic sifat
charcoal arang
chart rajah; carta
chase, to kejar, mengejar
chase away, chase out usir, mengusir; halau, menghalau
chat cakap; celoteh; sembang
cheap murah
cheap sale jualan murah
cheat, to tipu, menipu; curang
cheat (someone who cheats) penipu
check (verify) semak; periksa
checked (pattern) corak
cheek pipi
cheeky nakal
cheerful gembira; riang
cheese keju
chess catur
chest (box) peti; kotak
chest (breast) dada
chew, to mengunyah
chicken ayam
chief ketua; penghulu
child anak
child (young person) kanak-kanak; budak
chili lada; cili
chili powder serbuk lada; serbuk cili
chili sauce sambal
chilled disejukkan
chin dagu
China negeri Cina
Chinese orang Cina; orang Tionghua
chocolate coklat
choice pilihan
cholera taun
choose, to pilih, memilih
chopsticks sepit
Christian penganut Kristian

Christianity agama Kristian
church gereja
cigar cerut
cigarette rokok
cinema panggung wayang; pawagam
cinnamon kulit kayu manis
circle lingkaran; bulatan
citizen warganegara; rakyat
city kota; bandar raya
city hall dewan bandar raya
clarify, to menjelaskan
class (at school) darjah
class (at university) kuliah
class (category) golongan
clean, to bersih, membersih
clear (of weather) cerah; terang
clear-cut jelas, terang
clerk kerani
clever cerdik; pintar
client pelanggan
climate iklim
climb onto, into naik
climb up (hills, mountains) daki, mendaki
clock jam
clog terompah
close, to tutup, menutup
close to (nearby) dekat; berhampiran
close together (tight) rapat
closed tutup
cloth kain
clothes, clothing pakaian
cloud awan
cloudy (overcast) mendung
clove bunga cengkih
coach (of train) gerabak
coast pantai
coastline tepi laut
coat (jacket) jaket
coat (overcoat) kot panjang
cobra ular senduk
cock ayam jantan
cockroach lipas
coconut kelapa

C

coconut milk santan
coffee kopi
coin duit syiling
cold dingin; sejuk
cold (flu) selsema; flu
colleague (co-worker) rakan kerja
collect, to kutip, mengutip
collide, to tempuh, menempuh; langgar, melanggar
color warna
comb sikat
combine menggabung
come, to datang
come back kembali; pulang
come in masuk
come on! ayo!; mari!; jom!
comfortable selesa
command (order) perintah
commemorate mengingati
commerce perdagangan
commission suruhanjaya
committee jawatankuasa
common (frequent) sering
community masyarakat
compact disc cakera padat
companion rakan; sahabat; kawan; teman
company (firm) syarikat; perusahaan
compare, to membandingkan
compared with dibandingkan dengan
compartment petak
compensation ganti rugi
compete, to saing, bersaingan; tanding, bertanding
competition saingan; tandingan
complaint aduan
complete (finished) habis; selesai
complete (thorough) teliti
complete (whole) lengkap
completely sama sekali

complexion wajah; kulit muka
complicated rumit
compliment puji, pujian
compose menulis; mengarang; menggubah
composition (writings) karangan
comprise mengandungi
compromise, to tolak ansur, bertolak ansur
compulsory wajib
computer komputer
concentrate, to (thoughts) meumpukan fikiran
concerned bimbang; khuatir; mengambil berat
concerning tentang; mengenai; berkenaan
concise ringkas; pendek
conclusion tamat; selesai
condition (pre-condition) syarat
condition (status) keadaan
condolence takziah
confectionery gula-gula
conference persidangan
confide mengadu; mencurah perasaan
confidence kepercayaan; keyakinan
confidential sulit; rahsia
confirm, to mengesahkan
confiscate, to rampas, merampas
Confucianism ideologi orang Cina
confuse, to keliru, mengeliru
confused (in a mess) kacau
confused (mentally) bingung
confusing membingungkan
congested penuh sesak
congratulations! syabas! tahniah!
connect together, to sambung, menyambung
conscious sedar
consent persetujuan; keizinan

consider (have an opinion) fikir, berfikiran

consider (think over) timbang, mempertimbang

considerable banyak

considerate bertimbang rasa

consist of mengandungi

constant tetap; sentiasa

consult (talk over with) runding, berunding

consultant pakar runding

contact (connection) hubungan

contact (get in touch with) hubungi, menghubungi

contain mengandungi

container bekas

content berpuas hati

continent benua

continue, to teruskan, meneruskan; bersambung

contract perjanjian; kontrak

convenient mudah; senang; selesa

conversation percakapan

cook (person) tukang masak

cook, to masak, memasak

cooked sudah masak

cooker (stove) dapur

cookie (sweet biscuit) biskut

cooking (cuisine) masakan

cool sejuk

cooperate bekerjasama

copper tembaga

copy salinan

copyright hakcipta

coral batu karang

corn (grain) jagung

corner sudut; penjuru

correct, to betul, membetulkan

correspond (write letters) surat-menyurat

corridor lorong; koridor

cost (expense) kos

cost (price) harga

cotton kapas

cough batuk

could (might) mungkin

count, to kira, menggira

counter (for paying, buying tickets) tempat membayar; kaunter

country (nation) negara

country (rural area) desa

court mahkamah

courteous sopan

courtyard halaman dalam

cousin sepupu

cover, to tutup, menutup; tudung, menudung

cow lembu

co-worker (colleague) rakan sejawat

crab ketam

cracked retak

cracker (salty biscuit) kraker

craft kraf

craftsperson tukang

crate peti

crazy gila

create, to cipta, mencipta; buat, membuat

creature makhluk

criminal penjahat

cross (angry) marah

cross (go over) menyeberang

crowded penuh sesak

cruel kejam; bengis; zalim

cry, to tangis, menangis

cry out, to teriak, berteriak

cucumber timun

cuisine (style of cooking) santapan

culture kebudayaan

cup cawan

cupboard almari; gerobok

cure (medical) ubat; sembuh

cured (preserved) diawetkan

currency mata wang

curtains (drapes) langsir

custom (tradition) adat

customer pelanggan

cut, to potong, memotong

D D

daddy abah; ayah; bapa
daily setiap hari; harian
dam empangan
damage, to rosak, merosakkan
damp lembab; basah
dance tarian
danger bahaya
daring (brave) berani
dark gelap
date (of the month) tarikh; hari bulan
date of birth tarikh lahir
daughter anak perempuan
daughter-in-law menantu perempuan
dawn subuh; fajar
day hari
day after tomorrow lusa
day before yesterday kemarin
day off hari cuti
daydream, to angan-angan
daze binggung
dead mati
dead end jalan mati
deadline tarikh akhir
deaf pekak; tuli
dean (of university) dekan
dear yang disayangi
death kematian
debt hutang
deceive, to tipu, menipu
December Disember
decide, to putus, memutuskan
decline (get less) menurun
decline (refuse) menolak
decorate, to hias, menghiasi
decrease, to kurang, mengurangi
deduct potong; tolak
deep bahagian yang dalam
defeat, to kalah, mengalahkan
defecate, to buang air besar; berak

defect kecacatan; kerosakan
defer, to tangguh, menangguh
definite (certain) pasti; tetap
degree (level) peringkat; taraf
degree (temperature) darjat
degree (university) ijazah
delayed (late) terlambat
delayed (put off) menunda
delegate wakil
deliberate dengan sengaja
delicate halus; lemah lembut
delicacy makanan istimewa
delicious sedap; enak; lazat
delight seronok; gembira
deliver, to hantar, menghantar; kirim, mengirim
demand, to tuntut, menuntut
demonstrate, to tunjuk, menunjukkan
dentist doktor gigi
depart, to berangkat; bertolak; pergi
department jabatan; bahagian
department store kedai serbanika
depend on, to gantung, bergantung
deposit (put money in the bank) menabung
descendant keturunan
describe, to gambarkan, menggambarkan
desert (arid land) gurun; padang pasir
desert (to abandon) meninggalkan
design reka bentuk
designation pangkat
designer pereka
desire hajat; hasrat; idaman
desire, to ingin, keinginan
desk meja tulis
despite walaupun
dessert manisan
destination tujuan; destinasi
destiny takdir

D

destroy, to hancur, menghancur; binasa, membinasakan
detail butir-butir
detergent (for clothes) sabun cuci baju
detergent (for eating utensils) sabun cuci piring
determined (stubborn) berazam
develop, to (film) cuci, mencuci
develop, to (happen) berkembang
device alat
devout alim; warak
dew embun
diagonal pepenjuru; diagonal
diagram gambar rajah
dial, to (telephone) menelepon
diamond intan; berlian
diaper lampin
diary (daybook, journal) buku harian; diari
dictionary kamus
die, to mati; meninggal dunia
different berlainan; berbeza
different (other) yang lain
difficult susah; payah; sukar; sulit
dig, to gali, menggali
dignity maruah
dilute, to cair, mencairkan
dine makan
dinghy bot kecil
dining room bilik makan
dining table meja makan
dinner (evening meal) makan malam
dipper (ladle) gayung
direct (non-stop) langsung; terus-menerus
direction arah; hala
director (of company) pengarah
dirty kotor

disagree tidak setuju
disappear hilang
disappointed kecewa
disaster bencana
disciple pengikut
disconnected diputus; dipotong
discount potongan harga; diskaun
discomfort rasa tidak selesa
discourage tidak menggalakkan
discuss, to bincang, membincang
disease penyakit
dish (particular food) hidangan; masakan
dish (platter) piring; pinggan
diskette disket
dislike, to tidak suka
display, to pamer, mempamerkan
dispose membuang
distance jarak
district daerah; wilayah; kawasan
disturb, to ganggu, mengganggu
ditch parit; longkang
dive (into sea) menyelam
diverse beraneka jenis
divide (split up) membahagikan
divorce, to cerai, bercerai
dizzy pening
do (perform an action) membuat; melakukan
doctor doktor
document dokumen
dog anjing
doll anak patung
dome (of mosque) kubah
donate menderma; menyumbang
done (cooked) masak
done (finished) selesai
don't! jangan!

D

door pintu
dose sukatan
dot titik
double (two times) dua kali ganda
doubt was-was; ragu-ragu
down (downward) turun
downstairs (room) tingkat bawah
downtown pusat bandar
dozed off terlelap
drain parit; longkang
drapes (curtains) langsir
draw, to lukis, melukis
drawer laci
drawing gambar
dream, to mimpi, bermimpi
dress (frock) baju
dressed, to get pakai baju
drink (refreshment) minuman
drink, to minum
drive, to (vehicle) pandu, memandu
driver drebar; pemandu kereta
drizzle hujan renyai-renyai
drought kemarau
drown, to mati tenggelam
drowsy menggantuk
drug (medicine) ubat
drug (recreational) dadah
drugstore (pharmacy) farmasi; kedai ubat
drunk mabuk
dry, to mengeringkan
dry out (in the sun) jemur
duck itik
duplicate salinan
durian durian
during semasa
dusk senja
dust debu; habuk
dustbin tong sampah
Dutch orang Belanda
duty (import tax) cukai import
duty (responsibility) tugas; kewajipan
duty-free bebas cukai

E

each (every) setiap; tiap-tiap
ear telinga
earache sakit telinga
earlier (beforehand) dulu
early awal
early in the morning pagi-pagi
earn, to mencari nafkah; mendapat wang
earnings pendapatan
earrings anting-anting
earth (soil) tanah
earth (the world) bumi
earthquake gempa bumi
east timur
easy senang; mudah
eat, to makan
eclipse gerhana
economical cermat
economy ekonomi
edge tepi; pinggir; batas
edit menyunting
edition keluaran; edisi
editorial lidah pengarang
educate, to didik, mendidik
education pendidikan
eerie ngeri; menyeramkan
effect (result) kesan; akibat; hasil
effective berkesan
efficient cekap
effort usaha
effort, to make an berusaha
egg telur
egg white putih telur
egg yolk kuning telur
eggplant (aubergine) terong
eight lapan
eighteen lapan belas
eighty lapan puluh
either salah satu
either...or atau
elbow siku
election pilihanraya

electric, electricity eletrik
electronic elektronik
elegant tampan; anggun
elephant gajah
elevator lift
eleven sebelas
elite golongan atasan; elit
else selain daripada itu
else; or else kalau tidak
elsewhere di tempat lain
email (message) emel
email (system) jaringan
  emel
email address alamat emel
embarrassed malu
embarrassing memalukan
embassy kedutaan besar
embrace, to peluk, memeluk
embroidery sulaman
emergency darurat;
  kecemasan
emotion perasaan; emosi
employ menggaji
employee pekerja
employer majikan
employment agency agensi
  pekerjaan
empty kosong
enclose menlampirkan;
  menyertakan
encourage, to galak,
  menggalakkan
encouragement galakan;
  dorongan
end (tip) hujung
end, to (finish) selesai; tamat
endanger membahayakan
endless tidak habis-habis
enemy musuh
energy tenaga; kuasa
engaged (telephone) sibuk
engaged (to be married)
  bertunang
engine mesin; enjin
engineer jurutera
England England
English orang Inggeris

engrave, to ukir, mengukir;
  pahat, memahat
enjoy, to bersuka-ria; nikmati,
  menikmati
enjoyable menyeronokkan
enlarge, to besarkan,
  membesarkan
enormous sangat besar
enough cukup
enquire, to tanya,
  menanya
enrol mendaftarkan nama
ensure menentukan
enter masuk
enterprise perusahaan
enterprising berdaya usaha
entertain menghiburkan;
  meraikan
entertainment hiburan
enthusiasm penuh semangat
enthusiast pengemar
entire seluruh
entirety (whole) keseluruhan
entrance (way in) pintu
  masuk
entrepreneur usahawan
envelope sampul surat
environment persekitaran;
  suasana
envious iri hati
envy cemburu; iri hati
equal seimbang; sama
equality kesamaan
Equator Khatulistiwa
equip melengkap
equipment kelengkapan;
  peralatan
equivalent sama
era zaman; masa; era
erase memadamkan
eraser pemadam
error kesalahan; kesilapan
erupt meletus
escalator eskalator
especially terutama; khusus
essay karangan
essence pati

E

E

essential mustahak; penting
establish (set up) mendirikan; menubuhkan
estate ladang; estet
estimate anggaran
ethnic group bangsa; suku bangsa
Europe Eropah
European orang Eropah
even (also) juga
even (smooth) rata
even if biarpun
even though sekalipun
evening petang
event peristiwa
eventually akhirnya
ever (have already) pernah
everlasting kekal
every setiap; segala
every kind of segala macam
every now and then sekali-sekala
every time tiap kali
everybody, everyone setiap orang
everything segala-galanya
everywhere di mana-mana
exact tepat
exam (test) ujian; peperiksaan
examine, to uji, mengguji; periksa, memeriksa
example contoh; umpama; misal
example, for umpamanya; misalnya
exceed melebihi
excellent cemerlang
except kecuali
exchange, to (money, opinions) tukar, menukar
exchange rate kadar pertukaran
excited gembira
exciting mengembirakan
excuse alasan
excuse me! (getting past) tumpang lalu!

exercise latihan
exercise (physical) senaman
exhausted sangat letih; kepenatan
exhibition pameran
exist, to ada
exit (way out) keluar
expand, to (grow larger) berkembang
expect, to harap, mengharapkan
expectant mother bakal ibu
expense belanja
expensive mahal
experience, to pengalaman, mengalami
experiment penyelidikan
expert pakar
expertise kemahiran; kepakaran
expire berakhir; tamat
explain, to menerangkan; menjelaskan
explanation penerangan; penjelasan
explore menjelajah
export, to eksport, mengeksport
express, to (state) ucapkan, mengucapkan
express (speed) segera; ekspres
extension (telephone) sambungan
external luar
extinct pupus
extinguisher pemadam api
extra (additional) tambahan
extraordinary luar biasa; istimewa
extravagant boros
extremely sangat
eye mata
eyebrow bulu kening
eyeglasses (spectacles) kacamata; cermin mata
eyelid kelopak mata

F

fabric (textile) kain
face muka; rupa; wajah
face, to hadapi, menghadapi
fact kenyataan
factory kilang
fade pudar; luntur
fail, to gagal
faint pitam
fair patut; baik; adil
faith kepercayaan; keyakinan
fake palsu; tiruan
fall (season) musim gugur;
  musim luruh
fall, to jatuh
fall for jatuh hati; terpikat
false (imitation) palsu; tiruan
false (not true) bohong
familiar biasa
family keluarga
famine kebuluran
famous terkenal; ternama
fan (admirer) peminat
fan (for cooling) kipas
fantastic luar biasa; sungguh
  bagus
far jauh
fare tambang perjalanan
farewell selamat tinggal
farm ladang; kebun
farmer petani
farther lebih jauh
fast (rapid) cepat; lekas
fast, to puasa, berpuasa
fat (grease) lemak
fat (plump) gemuk
fate nasib; takdir
father bapa; ayah; abah
father-in-law bapa mentua
fault kesalahan; kekurangan
favorite kegemaran; pilihan
fax (machine) mesin faks
fax (message) kiriman faks
fear ketakutan
fearless berani
feast kenduri; jamuan

feather bulu
February Februari
fee bayaran; yuran
feed, to memberi
  makan
feel, to rasa, merasa
feeling perasaan
female perempuan; wanita
fence pagar
ferry feri
fertile subur
festival perayaan; pesta
fetch, to ambil, mengambil
fever demam
few sedikit
fiancé tunang lelaki
fiancée tunang perempuan
field padang
fierce garang
fifteen lima belas
fifty lima puluh
figure (number) angka
fill, to isi, mengisi
film (camera, movie) filem
final terakhir
finally akhirnya
finance kewangan
find jumpa
find out mendapat tahu
fine (okay) baik
fine (punishment) denda
finger jari
fingernail kuku jari
fingerprint cap jari
finish off, to habiskan
finished (completed) selesai
finished (none left) habis
fire api
fire brigade pasukan bomba
fire someone, to pecat,
  pecatkan
firecracker mercun
fireman anggota bomba
fireworks bunga api
firm (company) syarikat
firm (definite) pasti
firm (mattress) keras

F

F

first pertama
fish ikan
fish pond kolam ikan
fish, to pancing, memancing
fish sauce sos ikan
fishing net jala; pukat
fit padan; sesuai; layak
five lima
fix, to (a time, appointment) menetapkan; menentukan
fix, to (repair) betulkan, membetulkan
flag bendera
flashlight (torch) lampu suluh
flat (apartment) rumah pangsa
flat (smooth) rata; datar
flavor perisa
flesh daging
flight penerbangan
flood banjir; bah
floor lantai
flour tepung
flower bunga
flu selsema
fluent fasih; lancar
fly (insect) lalat
fly, to terbang, menerbang
fold, to lipat, melipat
follow along, to ikut, mengikut
follower pengikut
fond of, to be sayang, menyayangi
food makanan
foolish bodoh
foot kaki
football bola sepak
for untuk; demi
forbid, to melarang
force, to paksa, memaksa
forecast ramalan
forefather nenek moyang
forehead dahi
foreigner orang asing
forest hutan
forever selamanya
forget, to lupa
forgive, to mengampun

fork garpu
form (shape) bentuk
form (to fill out) borang
former dahulu; bekas
fortnight dua minggu
fortunately nasib baik; mujurlah
fortune kekayaan
forty empat puluh
forward maju
fountain air pancut
four empat
fourteen empat belas
fragrant wangi; harum
France Perancis
free gift hadiah percuma
free of charge percuma
freedom kemerdekaan; kebebasan
freeze, to beku, membekukan
frequent sering
French orang Perancis
fresh segar
Friday Jumaat
fried goreng
friend kawan; teman; sahabat
friendly (outgoing) ramah; mesra
friendship persahabatan
frightened takut
from dari; daripada
front depan; muka
frozen beku
fruit buah
fry, to goreng, menggoreng
fulfill, to penuhi, memenuhi
full penuh
full (eaten one's fill) kenyang
fun, to have berseronok; bersuka-suka
funeral pengkebumian
fun-fair pesta ria
funny lucu
furniture perabot
fussy cerewet
futile sia-sia
future masa depan

G

gain menguntungkan
gale ribut
gamble, to judi, berjudi
game (toy) permainan
gangster penjahat
gap ruang
garage (for repairs) bengkel; garaj
garbage sampah
garden (yard) taman; kebun
gardener tukang kebun
garlic bawang putih
garment pakaian
gate pintu pagar
gather, to kumpul, mengumpul
gathering perhimpunan; perjumpaan
gay (happy) meriah; riang
gaze merenung
gem permata
gender jantina
general (all-purpose) umum
general knowledge pengetahuan am
general meeting mesyuarat agung
generally biasanya; umumnya
generation keturunan
generous murah hati
gentle lemah-lembut
genuine sebenar; asli; jati
germ kuman; hama
German orang Jerman
Germany negara Jerman
gesture (movement) gerak geri
get, to (receive) dapat, mendapat
get in masuk
get off (transport) turun
get on (transport) naik
get together berjumpa
get up (from bed) bangun

get well soon lekas sembuh
ghee minyak sapi
ghost hantu
giddy pening
gift hadiah
gifted berbakat
ginger halia
girl gadis; anak perempuan
girlfriend teman wanita
give, to beri, memberi
give and take tolak ansur
give in menyerah diri
given name nama asli
glad suka; gembira; riang
glance toleh
glare (from strong light) silau
glass (for drinking) gelas
glass (material) kaca
glasses (spectacles) kaca mata; cermin mata
global sedunia
glove sarung tangan
glow bercahaya
glue pelekat; gam
go, to pergi; jalan
go against menentang
go along (join in) ikut, mengikuti
go around (visit) kunjungi
go back balik
go for a walk jalan-jalan
go home pulang
go out (exit) keluar
go out (fire, candle) padam
go to bed tidur
go up (climb) naik
goal objective) tujuan
goat kambing
God Tuhan; Allah
gold emas; mas
gold chain rantai emas
goldsmith tukang emas
golf golf
gone (finished) habis
good baik; bagus; elok
goodbye (said to someone leaving) selamat jalan

G

G

goodbye (said to someone remaining) selamat tinggal
good-hearted baik hati
good-looking kacak (for male); cantik, jelita (for female)
goodness! alamak!
goods barang-barang
goose angsa
gorgeous sungguh cantik
government kerajaan
grab, to rebut, merebut; rampas, merampas
grade gred; peringkat
gradually sedikit demi sedikit
graduate siswazah
grain bijiran
grammar tatabahasa
grand (great) hebat; indah
grandchild cucu
granddaughter cucu perempuan
grandfather datuk
grandmother nenek
grandson cucu lelaki
grape buah anggur
graph rajah; graf
grass rumput
grateful berterima kasih; berhutang budi; bersyukur
grave kubur
gravestone batu nisan
gravy kuah; gulai
gray kelabu
great agung; hebat; sangat
greedy tamak; gelojoh
green hijau
green beans kacang buncis
greens sayur
greet, to sambut, menyambut; memberi salam
greetings salam; selamat sejahtara
greeting card kad ucapan
grief kesedihan
grill, to panggang, memanggang
grime kotoran; daki

grin, to tersengih-sengih
grind, to giling, menggiling
grinder pengasah
grindstone batu giling
gross kasar
gross income pendapatan kasar
grouch, to sungut, bersungut
ground (earth) tanah, bumi
ground (reason) sebab
groundless tidak berasas
groundnut kacang tanah
group rombongan; kumpulan; golongan; kelompok
grow (be growing, e.g. plant) tumbuh, bertumbuh
grow (cultivate) tanam, menanam
grow larger, to berkembang; membesar
grow up (child) tumbuh; berkembang
grown-up (adult) dewasa
grudge dendam; dengki
grumble, to sungut, bersungut
guarantee jaminan
guarantee, to jamin, menjamin
guard, to jaga, menjaga; kawal, mengawal
guardian penjaga
guess, to agak, mengagak; teka, meneka
guest tetamu
guesthouse rumah persinggahan
guestroom bilik tetamu
guest-of-honor tetamu khas
guidance bimbingan; pimpinan
guide, to (lead) pandu, memandu; pimpin, memimpin
guidebook buku panduan
guideline garis panduan
gum gam; pelekat
gum (of mouth) gusi**gun** senapang
gunfire tembakan
guy lelaki

H

habit tabiat
haggle tawar-menawar
hair rambut
hairbrush berus rambut
hairdresser pendandan rambut
hairstyle fesyen rambut
hairy berbulu
half setengah; separuh
half-cooked separuh masak
hall dewan
halt berhenti
hammer tukul
hand tangan
hand (of clock) jarum jam
handbag beg tangan
handbook buku panduan
handmade buatan tangan
handout pemberian
handwriting tulisan tangan
handicap cacat
handicraft kerja tangan
handkerchief sapu tangan
handle (bag) pemegang
handle (broom) tangkai
handsome kacak
handy cekap
hang, to gantung, menggantung
happen (occur) terjadi
happening (incident) kejadian
happy bahagia; gembira
happy birthday! selamat ulang tahun!
happy new year! selamat tahun baru!
harbor pelabuhan
hard (difficult) sukar; sulit
hard (solid) keras
hard-headed keras kepala
hardship kesusahan
hardworking (industrious) rajin
harmful berbahaya
harmless tidak berbahaya

harvesting menuai
has ada; mempunyai
haste tergesa-gesa; terburu-buru
hat topi
hate, to benci, membenci
hatred kebencian
have, to (own) punya
have been somewhere ke suatu tempat
have done something melakukan sesuatu
have to (must) harus
haze jerebu
he, him dia; beliau
head kepala
head (leader) ketua; pemimpin
head for (toward) menuju
headache sakit kepala
headdress hiasan kepala
headquarters ibu pejabat
heal sembuh
healthy sihat
hear, to dengar, mendengar
heart jantung; hati
heart-broken patah hati
heart-warming mengharukan
heartless kejam
heat kepanasan
heat, to memanaskan
heavy berat
heel tumit
height ketinggian
heir waris
heirloom pusaka
helmet topi keledar
help! tolong!
help, to tolong, menolong; bantu, membantu
helper pembantu
helpless tidak berupaya
hem (of dress) kelim
her dia; beliau
here sini; di sini
heritage warisan
hero wira; tokoh
hers dia punya

H

hide, to sembunyi, menyembunyikan; sorok, menyorok
high tinggi
highlight acara kemuncak
highly sangat; amat
highway lebuh raya
hill bukit
hillside lereng bukit
hinder, to halang, menghalang
hindrance halangan
hip tulang rusuk
hire, to (a car) sewa, menyewa
hire, to (a person) upah, mengupah
hire-purchase sewa-beli
his dia punya
history sejarah
historic bersejarah
history sejarah
hit, to (strike) pukul, memukul
hoax penipuan
hobby kegemaran; hobi
hold, to (grasp) pegang, memegang
hold back menahan diri
hole lubang
holiday (festival) kelepasan
holiday (vacation) cuti
holy suci
home (house) rumah
honest jujur
honey madu
honeymoon bulan madu
honor harga diri
honor, to memberi kehormatan
hope, to harap, berharap
hopefully mudah-mudahan
horizontal melintang
horn (of animal) tanduk
horrible dasyat
horse kuda
hospital rumah sakit; hospital
host tuan rumah; hos
hostel asrama; hostel
hot (spicy) pedas

hot (temperature) panas
hot air (talk) cakap besar
hot spring mata air panas
hotel hotel
hour jam; waktu
house rumah
housemaid orang gaji
housewife suri rumah tangga
housework kerja rumah
housing perumahan
how? bagaimana? macam mana?
how are you? apa khabar?
how long? berapa lama?
how many/much? berapa?
how old? (object) berapa usianya?
how old? (person) berapa umurnya?
however bagaimanapun
hub pusat
huge sangat besar
human being manusia
human nature tabiat manusia
human rights hak asasi manusia
humanity kemanusiaan
humble rendah diri; tidak sombong
humid lembap
humiliate memalukan
humorus lucu; kelakar
hundred ratus
hundred thousand seratus ribu
hungry lapar
hurricane ribut; taufan
hurry cepat; lekas
hurt (injured) luka, terluka; cedera, tercedera
hurt, to (cause pain) sakit, menyakiti
husband suami; laki
husk sabut
hut (shack) pondok
hygienic bersih
hypermarket pasar besar

I

I saya; aku
ice ais; air batu
ice cream ais krim
idea fikiran; idea
identical sama; serupa
identity card kad pengenalan
idol berhala
if kalau; jika; sekiranya
ignore, to tidak peduli
ignorant tidak tahu; jahil
ill (sick) sakit
illegal tidak sah
illiterate buta huruf
illness penyakit
immediately serta-merta;
  dengan segera
impatient tidak sabar
impolite tidak sopan
import, to import, mengimport
important penting; mustahak
impossible mustahil; tidak
  mungkin
impressive menarik; hebat
improve memperbaiki
in (space) di
in (time, years) pada
in order that (so that) agar;
  supaya
inch inci
incident kejadian; peristiwa
including termasuk
income gaji; pendapatan
inconsiderate tidak
  bertimbang rasa
inconvenient tidak sesuai
incorrect tidak betul
increase, to tambah,
  bertambah; tambah banyak
independent bebas; merdeka
indication tanda
indifferent tidak peduli
indigenous asli
indigestion senak; sakit perut
individual perseorangan;
  individu

indoor dalam rumah
inexpensive murah
infant bayi; anak kecil
infection jangkitan
influenza demam selsema
inform, to beritahu,
  memberitahukan; terangkan
information keterangan;
  maklumat
ingredient ramuan; bahan
inhabitant penduduk;
  penghuni
initially pada mulanya; mula-
  mula
inject, to suntik; menyuntik
injury luka; kecederaan
insect serangga
inside dalam
inspect, to periksa, memeriksa
instead of sebaliknya
instruct (tell to do something)
  suruh, menyuruh
insult, to hina, menghina
intend, to hendak;
  bermaksud; bertujuan
interesting menarik
interpreter penterjemah
intersection simpangan
into ke dalam
invent, to cipta, mencipta
invite, to (ask along) ajak,
  mengajak
invite, to (formally) undang
invoice invois
involve, to libat, melibatkan
iron besi
iron, to (clothing) gosok,
  menggosok
Islam agama Islam
island pulau
ivory gading

J

jacket jaket
jail penjara
jam jem

J

January Januari
Japan Jepun
Japanese orang Jepun
jaw rahang
jealous cemburu; iri hati
jewelry barang-barang kemas
job pekerjaan; tugas
joke bergurau; bersenda
journalist wartawan
journey perjalanan
jug (pitcher) kendi
juice jus
July Julai
jump, to lompat, melompat
June Jun
jungle hutan
just (fair) adil
just (only) cuma; hanya; saja
just now baru saja; baru tadi
juvenile remaja

K

keen berminat
keep, to simpan, menyimpan
keep away menjauhkan diri
keep it up teruskan
keep out di larang masuk
kettle cerek
key (to room) kunci
kick, to tendang, menendang
kid budak; anak kambing
kidney ginjal; buah pinggang
kin saudara-mara
kind (affectionate) baik hati
kind (type) macam; jenis
king raja
kiss, to cium, mencium
kitchen dapur
kite layang-layang; wau
knee lutut
knife pisau
knock, to ketuk, mengetuk
know (be acquainted with) kenal, mengenal
know (be informed) tahu
knowledge pengetahuan

L

labor buruh
lack kekurangan
lad pemuda; budak lelaki
ladder tangga
ladle (dipper) gayung
lady wanita; perempuan
lake tasik
lamb (mutton) daging kambing; daging biri-biri
lamp lampu
land tanah
landslide tanah runtuh
lane (alley) lorong
language bahasa
large besar
last terakhir
last night malam tadi; semalam
last week minggu yang lalu
last year tahun yang lalu
late terlambat; terlewat
late at night larut malam
later nanti
laugh ketawa; gelak
laws undang-undang
lawyer peguam
layer lapisan
lay the table siapkan meja makan
lazy malas
lead (be a leader) memimpin
lead (guide someone somewhere) menunjuk jalan
leader pemimpin
leaf daun
leak bocor
learn belajar
kecil; paling sedikit
least (at least) sekurang-kurangnya
least (smallest amount) paling
leather kulit
leave (depart) pergi; berangkat; tinggal
lecture ceramah; kuliah

ecturer (at university)
  pensyarah
eft (hand side) kiri
eft (remaining) baki; sisa;
  tinggal
eg kaki
egal sah
emon (citrus) lemon
emongrass serai
end, to pinjam, meminjamkan
ength panjangnya
ess (smaller amount, minus)
  kurang
essen (reduce) mengurangi
esson pelajaran
et (allow) biar, membiarkan
et someone know beritahu
etter surat
evel (even, flat) rata
evel (height) ketinggian
evel (standard) nilai
ibrary perpustakaan
icense (for driving) lesen
  memandu
icense (permit) permit
ick, to jilat, menjilat
id tudung; penutup
ie, to (tell a falsehood)
  bohong, membohong
ie down baring
ife nyawa
ifetime seumur hidup
ift (elevator) lif
ift (raise) angkat, mengangkat
ift (ride in car) menupang
ight (bright) terang
ight (lamp) lampu
ight (not heavy) ringan
ighter pemetik api
ightning kilat
ike (as) seperti
ike (be pleased by) suka
ike that begitu
ime (citrus) limau nipis
ine (mark) garis
ine (queue) barisan
ine up, to beratur; berbaris

lip bibir
lipstick gincu
liquid cecair
liquor (alcohol) alkohol
list daftar; senarai
listen, to dengar, mendengar
literature sastera,
  kesusasteraan
little (not much) sedikit
little (small) kecil
live (be alive) hidup
live (stay in a place) tinggal;
  diam
live-in tinggal bersama
liver hati
lizard cicak
load muatan
located, to be terletak
lock kunci
lodge (small hotel) rumah
  pengginapan
lonely kesepian
long (size) panjang
long (time) lama
look! lihat!; lihatlah!
look (seem, appear)
  kelihatannya
look after mengawasi;
  menjaga
look at, see lihat, melihat
look for cari, mencari
look like mirip; serupa
look out! awas!
look up (find in book) cari
loose (wobbly) longgar
lose (be defeated) kalah
lose (mislay) hilang;
  kehilangan
lose money rugi
lost (can't find way) tersesat
lost (missing) hilang
lottery loteri
loud bising
love cinta; rasa sayang
lovely (person) cantik
lovely (thing) bagus
low rendah

L

lucky beruntung
luggage bagasi
lunch (midday meal) makan tengah hari
lungs paru-paru
luxurious mewah

M

machine mesin
madam (term of address) puan
magazine majalah
mail (post) surat
mail, to kirim surat, mengirim surat
main (most important) paling utama; paling penting
mainly sebahagian besar
major (important) penting; utama
make, to buat, membuat; bikin, membikin
male lelaki
man (human being) orang
man (male person) lelaki
manage (succeed) berhasil; berjaya
manager pengurus
mango mangga
manufacture, to buat, membuat
many banyak
map peta
March Mac
margarine mentega
market pasar
marry berkahwin; menikah
mask topeng
massage, to urut, mengurut
mat tikar
match (game) pertandingan
matches mancis
material (ingredient) bahan
matter (issue) soal; hal
mattress tilam

May Mei
may boleh
maybe mungkin
mean (cruel) kejam; bengis
mean (intend) bertujuan
meaning erti; maksud
meanwhile sementara itu
measure, to ukur, mengukur
meat daging
meatball berbola daging
medical perubatan
medicine ubat
meet, to temu, bertemu; jumpa, berjumpa
meeting mesyuarat; pertemuan; perjumpaan
melon tembikai
member anggota
memories kenang-kenangan
mend, to perbaiki, memperbaiki
menstruate, to haid; datang bulan
mention, to sebut, menyebut
menu menu
merely cuma; hanya
message pesanan
metal logam; besi
method cara
midday tengah hari
middle (be in the middle of doing) sedang
middle (center) tengah
midnight tengah malam
mild (not severe) ringan; sedikit
mild (not spicy) tidak pedas
milk susu
million juta
mind (brain) otak
minibus bas mini
minor (not important) perkara kecil; masalah kecil
minute (size) sangat kecil
minute (time) minit
mirror cermin
misfortune nasib tak baik

miss, to (loved one) rindu
missing hilang
mist kabus
mistake kesalahan; kesilapan
misunderstanding salah
  faham
mix, to campur, mencampur
mobile phone telepon bimbit
modern moden
modest (simple) sederhana
moment (instant) saat
moment (just a moment)
  sebentar
Monday Isnin
money wang; duit
monkey monyet; kera
month bulan
monument tugu
moon bulan
more (comparative) lebih
more of (things) lagi; lebih
  banyak
more or less lebih kurang
morning pagi
mosque masjid
mosquito nyamuk
most (superlative) paling
most (the most of) paling
  banyak; terbanyak
mostly kupu-kupu
moth ngengat
mother ibu
mother-in-law ibu mertua;
  mak mertua
motor (engine) enjin
motor vehicle kereta;
  kenderaan
motorcycle motorsikal
mountain gunung
mouse tikus
moustache misai
mouth mulut
move, to gerak, bergerak
move from one place to
  another pindah, memindah
movie filem
muscle otot

mushroom cendawan
music muzik
Muslim penganut Islam;
  Muslim
must harus; mesti
my saya

N

nail (finger, toe) kuku
nail (spike) paku
naked telanjang
name nama
narrow sempit
nation (country) negara
national nasional
nationality kebangsaan
natural semulajadi
nature alam
naughty nakal
nearby dekat
nearly hampir
neat (orderly) rapi; teratur
necessary harus; mesti
neck leher
necklace rantai leher
necktie tali leher
need keperluan
need, to perlu, memerlukan
needle jarum
neighbor tetangga; jiran
neither mahupun
nephew anak saudara lelaki
nest sarang
net jaring
Netherlands, the negara
  Belanda
network jaringan
never tidak pernah
never mind! tidak apa!
nevertheless namun itu
new baru
news khabar; berita
newspaper surat khabar
next (in line, sequence)
  berikut

N

N

next to di samping;
di sebelah
next week minggu depan
next year tahun depan
nice (food) sedap; enak
nice (object) bagus
nice (person) baik
niece anak saudara
perempuan
night malam
nightclothes, nightdress baju
tidur
nightly tiap malam
nine sembilan
nineteen sembilan belas
ninety sembilan puluh
no, not (with nouns) bukan
**no, not (with verbs and
adjectives)** tidak
nobody tidak seorangpun
noise bunyi
noisy bising
nonsense cakap kosong; karut
non-stop langsung
noodles mee
noon siang
nor baik...maupun...tidak
normal biasa
normally biasanya
north utara
north-east timur laut
north-west barat laut
nose hidung
nostril lubang hidung
not tidak; bukan
not only...but also
baik...maupun
not yet belum
note (currency) wang kertas
note (written) nota
note down catat, mencatat
notebook buku catatan
nothing tidak ada apa-apa
notice pengumuman
notice, to memperhatikan
novel novel
November November

now sekarang
nowadays pada masa
sekarang
nowhere tidak dimanapun
nude telanjang
numb tidak terasa; rasa semut
number nomber
nurse jururawat
nylon nilon

O

o'clock jam; pukul
obedient patuh; turut
obey, to turut, menurut
object (thing) benda; barang;
objek
object, to (protest)
membantah; membangkang
occasionally kadang-kadang
occupation pekerjaan
ocean laut
October Oktober
odor (bad smell) bau
of (from) dari
of course memang
off (gone bad) busuk
off (to turn something off)
memadamkan; mematikan
offend, to menyakitkan hati;
menyinggung perasaan
offer, to (suggest)
menawarkan
offering tawaran; sajian
office pejabat
official (formal) rasmi
officials (government)
pegawai kerajaan
often sering
oil minyak
okay (yes, uninjured) okay;
baik
old (person) tua
old (thing) lama; tua
olden times, in pada zaman
dulu

older brother abang
older sister kakak
omelette telur dadar
on (at) di
on (date) pada
on (to turn something on) hidupkan; nyalakan; jalankan
on (turned on) nyala; hidup; jalan
on board sudah naik
on fire terbakar
on foot jalan kaki
on the whole pada umumnya; pada keseluruhannya
on time tepat waktu
once sekali
one satu; se-
one-way ticket tiket untuk satu arah saja
one who (the one which) yang
onion bawang
only saja; cuma; hanya
open terbuka
open, to buka, membuka
opinion pendapat
opponent lawan
opportunity kesempatan
oppose, to melawan
opposed (in opposition) berlawanan; bertentangan
opposite (contrary) malah
opposite (facing) menghadap
optional pilihan
or atau
orange (citrus) oren
orange (color) jingga
order (command) perintah
order (placed for food, goods) pesanan
order (sequence) susunan
order, to (command) perintah, memerintah
order something, to pesan, memesan
orderly (organized) teratur; rapi

organize, to (arrange) mengatur; mengurus; menyelenggarakan
origin asal
original asli
originate, to (come from) berasal dari
ornament hiasan
other lain
ought to seharusnya
our (excludes the one addressed) kami
our (includes the one addressed) kita
out luar
outside luar; di luar
outside of di luar
oval (shape) bujur telur
over (finished) selesai
over there di sana; di situ
over (to turn something over) balik
overcast (cloudy) mendung
overcome, to mengatas
overseas luar negera
overturned terbalik
owe, to hutang, berhutang
own (personal) milik sendiri
own, on one's sendirian
own, to memiliki; mempunyai
oyster tiram

P

pack, to bungkus, membungkus
package bungkus; paket
page halaman; muka surat
paid dibayar
pain perasaan sakit
painful sakit
paint cat
paint, to (a painting) melukis
paint, to (houses, furniture) cat, mengecat

P

P

painting lukisan
pair of, a sepasang
pajamas pijama; baju tidur
palace istana
pan kuali
panorama pemandangan
panties seluar dalam
pants seluar
paper kertas
parcel paket
pardon me? (what did you say?) apa?
parents orang tua; ibu bapa
park taman
park, to (car) meletak kereta
part (not whole) bahagian
part (spare) barang ganti
participate, to ikut, mengikuti; serta, menyertai; mengambilbahagiani
particularly (especially) khususnya
partly sebahagian
partner (in business) rakan kongsi
partner (in life, female) isteri
partner (in life, male) suami
party (event) pesta
party (political) parti
pass, to (exam) lulus
pass, to (go past) lalu
passenger penumpang
passport pasport
past (former) yang dahulu
past (go past) lewat
patient (calm) sabar
patient (doctor's) pesakit
pattern (design) corak
patterned bercorak
pawpaw papaya
pay, to bayar, membayar
pay attention perhatikan, memperhatikan
payment pembayaran
peace perdamaian
peaceful damai
peak (summit) puncak

peanut kacang tanah
pearl mutiara
peas kacang pis
peel, to kupas, mengupas
pen pen
pencil pensel
penis kemaluan lelaki; zakar
people orang ramai
pepper (black) lada hitam
pepper (chili) cili
pepper (white) lada putih
per cent peratus
percentage peratusan
performance pertunjukan
perfume minyak wangi
perhaps (maybe) mungkin
perhaps (probably) barangkali
period (end of a sentence) detik
period (menstrual) haid; datang bulan
period (of time) jangka masa; tempoh masa
permanent tetap
permit (license) permit
permit, to (allow) benar, membenarkan
person orang
personality watak
perspire, to peluh, berpeluh
pet animal binatang peliharaan
petrol petrol; minyak
petrol station stesen petrol; stesen minyak
pharmacy (drugstore) farmasi
Philippines, the Filipina
photocopy fotokopi
photocopy, to membuat salinan
photograph foto; gambar
photograph, to mengambil gambar
pick, to (choose) pilih, memilih
pick up (someone) jemput, menjemput

pick up, lift (something) angkat, mengangkat
pickpocket penyeluk saku
picture gambar
piece (item) barang
piece (portion, section) bahagian
pierce, to (penetrate) tembus, menembus
pig babi
pillow bantal
pill pil
pineapple nanas
pink merah muda
pitcher (jug) kendi
pity (what a pity!) sayangnya!
place tempat
place, to (put) taruh; tempatkan, menempatkan
plain (level ground) tanah rata
plain (not fancy) sederhana
plan, to rancang, merancang
plane pesawat; kapal terbang
plant tanaman
plant, to tanam, menanam
plastic plastik
plate piring
play, to main, memain
play around main-main
plead, to pohon, memohon
pleasant menyenangkan
please (go ahead) silakan; mari
please (request for help) tolong
please (request for something) minta
pleased senang hati
plug (bath) penyumbat
plug (electric) plag
plus tambah
pocket saku; poket
point (in time) saat
point out menunjuk
poison racun
police polis
police officer pegawai polis

polish, to gilap, menggilap; gosok, menggosok
polite sopan
politician ahli politik
politics politik
pond kolam
pool kolam
poor miskin
popular popular
porch serambi; anjung
pork daging babi
porridge bubur
port pelabuhan
portion (of food) bahagian
possess, to milik, memiliki; punya, mempunyai
possessions barang milik
possible, possibly mungkin
post (column) tiang
post, to (mail) kirim, mengirim
post office pejabat pos
postcard poskad
postpone, to tunda, menunda
postponed (delayed) tertunda, ditunda
pot periuk
potato kentang
poultry ayam
pour, to tuang, menuang
power kuasa; kekuatan
powerful berkuasa; kuat
practice latihan
practice, to berlatih, melatih
praise, to pujian, memuji
prawn udang
pray, to sembahyang, bersembahyang
prayer doa
prefer, to lebih suka
pregnant hamil
prepare, to (make ready) siapkan
prepared (ready) siap
prescription preskripsi
present (gift) hadiah
present (here) hadir

P

present, to beri, memberi
presently (nowadays) sekarang; kini
present moment, at the pada saat ini; sekarang
president presiden
press (journalism) wartawan
press, to tekan, menekan
pressure tekanan
pretend, to pura-pura, berpura-pura
pretty (considerably, very) agak, sangat
pretty (thing, place) indah
pretty (woman) cantik
prevent, to cegah, mencegah
price harga
pride rasa harga diri
priest paderi
print, to cetak, mencetak
prison penjara
private peribadi
probably barangkali
problem masalah
produce, to buat, membuat; hasil, menghasilkan
profession profesyen
profit untung
program (schedule) acara
promise, to janji, berjanji
pronounce, to ucap, mengucap
property tanah milik
protest, to bantah, membantah
proud bangga
prove, to bukti, membuktikan
public umum
publish, to terbit, menerbitkan
pull, to tarik, menarik
pump pam
punctual tepat pada waktu
pupil murid
pure tulen; jernih
purple unggu
purse (for money) dompet; beg duit

push, to dorong, mendorong
put, to (place) taruh, menaruh
put off (delay) menunda
put on (clothes) pakai
puzzled bingung

Q

qualification kelayakan
quality mutu
quarrel bertengkar
quarter seperempat; suku
queen ratu
queer ganjil
question pertanyaan
queue barisan
quick cepat
quickly dengan cepat
quiet sepi
quit (a job) letak jawatan
quit (stop) berhenti
quite (fairly) agak
quite (very) sangat

R

race bangsa
radio radio
rail (by rail) naik kereta api
railroad, railway landasan kereta api
rain, to rain hujan
raise, to (children) asuh, mengasuh
raise, to (lift) angkat, mengangkat
rank (station in life) pangkat
ranking kedudukan
rare (scarce) pelik; jarang jumpa
rare (uncooked) mentah
rarely (seldom) jarang
rat tikus
rate (tariff) kadar

R

rate of exchange (for foreign currency) kadar pertukaran
rather (fairly) agak
rather than daripada
raw (uncooked, rare) mentah
reach (get to) sampai; mencapai
react, to bertindak balas
reaction (response) tindak balas; reaksi
read, to baca, membaca
ready siap
ready, to get bersiap
ready, to make siapkan, menyiapkan
realize (be aware of) sedar, menyedari
really (in fact) kebetulan
really (very) amat; sangat
really? ya?
rear (tail) buntut
reason alasan; sebab
reasonable (price) berpatutan
reasonable (sensible) munasabah
receipt resit
receive, to terima, menerima
recipe resepi
recognize, to kenal, mengenal
recommend, to syor, mengesyorkan
recovered (cured) sembuh
rectangle segi empat
red merah
reduce, to kurang, mengurangi
reduction penurunan; pengurangan
reflect, to mencerminkan
refrigerator peti sejuk
refusal penolakan
refuse, to tolak, menolak
regarding terhadap; mengenai
region daerah
register, to daftar, mendaftar

registered letter surat berdaftar
regret, to menyesal
regrettably dengan kesal
regular (normal) biasa
relatives (family) keluarga; saudara
relax, to santai, bersantai; beristirehat
release, to lepas, melepaskan
religion agama
remainder (leftover) sisa; baki
remember, to ingat
remind, to mengingatkan
rent, to sewa, menyewa
rent out sewakan, menyewakan
repair, to betul, membetulkan; memperbaiki
repeat, to ulang, mengulangi
replace, to ganti, mengganti
reply (response) balasan; jawapan
reply, to (in speech) menjawab
reply, to (in writing or deeds) membalas
report laporan
report, to lapor, melapor
reporter wartawan
request, to (formally) mohon, memohon
request, to (informally) minta, meminta
rescue, to menyelamatkan
research penelitian; penyelidikan
research, to selidiki, menyelidiki
resemble, to mirip
reservation tempahan
reserve (for animals) tanah simpanan
reserve, to (ask for in advance) tempah
resident (inhabitant) penduduk

ENGLISH—BAHASA MALAYSIA

R

resolve, to (a problem) mengatasi; membereskan

respect hormat

respond (react) bertindak balas

response (reaction) reaksi; tindak balas

responsibility kewajipan; tanggungjawab

responsible, to be bertanggungjawab

rest (remainder) sisa; lebihan

rest, to (relax) istirehat

restaurant restoran

restrain, to tahan, tahankan

restroom bilik air

result akibat; hasil

resulting from disebabkan oleh; kerana

retired bersara

return (give back) mengembalikan

return (go back) kembali; balik

return home, to pulang

return ticket tiket pergi-pulang

reveal (make known) mengumumkan

reveal (make visible) menunjukkan

reverse, to (back up) undur

reversed (backwards) terbalik

ribbon pita; reben

rice (cooked) nasi

rice (plant) padi

rice (uncooked grains) beras

rice fields sawah padi

rich kaya

rid (get rid of) buang, membuang

ride, to ride (transport, animal) naik

right (correct) betul; benar

right (hand side) kanan

right now sekarang juga

rights hak

ring (jewelry) cincin

ring, to (bell) bunyikan

ring, to (on the telephone) menelefon

ripe matang; masak

rise, to (ascend) naik

rise, to (increase) naik

rival lawan

river sungai

road jalan

roasted (grilled, toasted) bakar; panggang

robe jubah

rock batu

role peranan

roof atap

room (in building) bilik

room (space) ruang

root (of plant) akar

rope tali

rotten busuk

rough kasar

roughly (approximately) kira-kira; lebih kurang

round (around) berkeliling

round (shape) bulat

rubber getah

rude tidak sopan; kasar

rules peraturan

run, to lari, melari

run away melarikan diri

S

sacred suci; keramat

sacrifice, to korban, mengorbankan

sad . sedih

safe selamat

sail, to layar, berlayar

salary gaji

sale, for untuk dijual

sale (reduced prices) jualan murah

sales assistant pembantu kedai

salt garam
salty masin
same sama
sample contoh; sampel
sand pasir
sandals selipar
satisfied puas
satisfy, to memuaskan
Saturday Sabtu
sauce sos
sauce (chili) sos cili
save, to (keep) simpan
save money (on a purchase) menjimat
say, to kata, berkata, mengatakan
say sorry minta maaf
say thank you terima kasih; mengucapkan terima kasih
scales dacing
scarce sukar didapati
scared takut
scenery pemandangan
schedule jadual
school sekolah
schoolchild murid
science sains
scissors gunting
screen (of computer) skrin komputer
scrub, to gosok, menggosok
sculpt, to ukir, mengukir
sculpture ukiran
sea laut
seafood makanan laut
search for cari, mencari
season musim
seat tempat duduk
second kedua
secret rahsia
secret, to keep a merahsiakan
secretary setiausaha
secure (safe) aman; selamat
see, to lihat, melihat
see you later! jumpa lagi!
seed biji
seek, to cari, mencari

seem, to rupa-rupanya
seldom jarang
select, to pilih, memilih
self diri; sendiri
sell, to jual, menjual
send, to kirim, mengirim
sensible berakal
sentence ayat
separate terpisah
separate, to pisah, memisahkan
September September
sequence (order) aturan
serious (not funny) serius
serious (severe) parah
servant pembantu rumah; orang gaji
serve, to layan, melayani
service layanan
sesame oil minyak bijan
sesame seeds biji bijan
set (of items) set
seven tujuh
seventeen tujuh belas
seventy tujuh puluh
several beberapa
severe parah
sew, to jahit, menjahit
sex (gender) jantina
sex (sexual activity) seks
shack pondok
shade teduh
shadow bayang
shadow play wayang kulit
shake, to goyang, bergoyang
shall (will) akan
shallow cetek
shame (disgrace) rasa malu
shame (what a shame!) sayang!
shampoo syampu
shape bentuk
shape, to (form) membentuk
shark ikan yu
sharp tajam
shave, to cukur, mencukur
she dia

S

sheep kambing biri-biri
sheet (for bed) cadar
sheet (of paper) sehelai
ship kapal
shiny berkilat
shirt baju; kemeja
shiver, to gigil, menggigil
shoes sepatu; kasut
shoot, to tembak, menembak
shop (go shopping) belanja, berbelanja
shop (store) kedai
shopkeeper pemilik kedai
short (concise) ringkas; pendek
short (not tall) pendek
short time (a moment) sebentar
shorts (short trousers) seluar pendek
shorts (underpants) seluar dalam
shoulder bahu
shout, to teriak, berteriak
show (broadcast) siaran
show (live performance) pertunjukan
show, to menunjukkan
shower (for washing) tempat mandi
shower (of rain) hujan
shower, to take a mandi
shrimp (prawn) udang
shut, to tutup, menutupi
sibling (older brother) abang
sibling (older sister) kakak
sibling (younger) adik
sick (ill) sakit
sick, to be (vomit) muntah
side samping
sightseeing makan angin; melancung
sign (symbol) tanda; petunjuk
sign, to menandatangani
signature tandatangan
signboard papan tanda

silent diam; sepi
silk sutera
silver perak
similar mirip
simple (easy) senang; mudah
simple (uncomplicated, modest) sederhana
since sejak
sing, to nyanyi, bernyani
Singapore Singapura
single (not married) bujang
single (only one) satu-satunya
sir (term of address) tuan
sister kakak
sister-in-law kakak ipar
sit, sit down duduk
situated, to be terletak
situation keadaan
six enam
sixteen enam belas
sixty enam puluh
size ukuran
skewer pencucuk
skillful mahir
skin kulit
skirt skirt
sky langit
sleep, to tidur
sleepy ngantuk
slender langsing; kurus
slight, slightly sedikit
slim langsing; kurus
slip (petticoat, underskirt) baju dalam
slippers selipar
slope lerengan
slow pelan; lambat
slowly pelan-pelan
small kecil
smart pandai; pintar
smell (bad odor) bau
smell, to cium, mencium
smile, to senyum, bersenyum
smoke asap

smoke, to (tobacco) merokok
smooth (surface) rata
smooth (unproblematic) lancar
smuggle, to seledup, menyeledup
snake ular
sneeze, to bersin
snow, to salji
soak, to rendam, merendam
soap sabun
soccer bola sepak
socket (electric) soket
socks stoken
sofa (couch) sofa
soft empuk; lembut; lembik
sold dijual
sold out habis
soldier askar; perajurit
sole (only) tunggal; satu-satunya
solid padat
solve, to (a problem) selesai, menyelesaikan
some beberapa
somebody, someone seseorang
something sesuatu
sometimes kadang-kadang
somewhere sesuatu tempat
son anak lelaki
son-in-law menantu lelaki
song lagu
soon segera
sore (painful) sakit
sorrow dukacita
sorry (to feel regretful) menyesal
sorry! ma'af!
sort (type) macam; jenis
sort out (deal with) membetulkan; memperbaiki
so that agar; supaya
sound (noise) bunyi
soup (clear) sup
soup (spicy stew) soto

sour masam
source sumber
south selatan
southeast tenggara
southwest barat daya
souvenir cenderamata
soy sauce (salty) kicap masin
soy sauce (sweet) kicap manis
space tempat; ruang
spacious luas; lapang
speak, to cakap, bercakap; kata berkata
special khusus; istimewa
spectacles cermin mata; kaca mata
speech ucapan
speech, to make a berucap
speed kecepatan; laju
spell, to eja, mengeja
spend, to belanja; membelanja
spices rempah-rempah
spicy pedas
spinach bayam; kangkung
spine tulang belakang
spiral spiral
spirits (hard liquor) alkohol; arak
spoiled (does not work) rosak
spoiled (food) busuk
spoon sudu
sponge span
sports sukan
spotted (pattern) berbintik-bintik
spray, to sembur; menyembur
spring (metal part) pegas
spring (of water) mata air
spring (season) musim bunga
square (shape) persegi
square (town square) medan
squid sotong
staff kakitangan; pekerja
stain kotoran
stairs tangga
stall (of vendor) warung; gerai

S

stall, to (car) tak bergerak
stamp (ink) cop
stamp (postage) setem
stand, stand up diri, berdiri
star bintang
start (beginning) permulaan
start, to mulai, memulai
stationery alat tulis
statue patung
stay, to (remain) tinggal
stay overnight menginap
steal, to curi, mencuri
steam wap
steamed kukus
steel keluli
steer, to memandu
step langkah
steps (stairs) tangga
stick (pole) batang
stick out tonjol, menonjol
stick to lekat, melekat
sticky melekit
stiff kaku
still (even now) masih
still (quiet) sepi; sunyi
stink, to bau, berbau
stomach (belly) perut
stone batu
stoop bongkok
stop (bus) perhentian bus
stop (train) stesen kereta api
stop, to (cease) berhenti; selesai
stop, to (halt) berhenti
stop by (pay a visit) melawat
store (shop) kedai
store, to simpan, menyimpan
storm taufan
story (of a building) tingkat
story (tale) cerita
stout (person) gemuk
stove (cooker) dapur
straight (not crooked) lurus
straight ahead terus
strait selat

strange aneh
stranger orang asing; orang luar
street jalan
strength kekuatan
strict tegas
strike, to go on mogok kerja
strike, to (hit) pukul, memukul
string tali
striped bergaris-garis
strong kuat
stubborn (determined) nekad; berazam
stuck (won't move) terlekat
student (school) murid
student (university) siswa
study, to belajar
stupid bodoh
style gaya
succeed, to berjaya
success kekjayaan
such (like that) seperti itu
such (quantity) amat; sangat
such as (for example) misalnya; umpamanya
suck, to hisap, menghisap
suddenly tiba-tiba
suffer, to sengsara; menderita
suffering kesengsaraan; penderitaan
sugar gula
sugarcane tebu
suggest, to cadang, mencadang
suggestion cadangan; usul
suit (clothes) sut
suitable (fitting, compatible) sesuai; cocok
suitcase beg baju
summer musim panas
summit (peak) puncak
sun matahari
Sunday Minggu; Ahad
sunlight sinar matahari
sunny cerah
sunrise matahari terbit

sunset matahari terbenam
supermarket pasar raya
supernatural power sakti
suppose, to anggap,
menganggap
sure pasti
surf ombak
surface permukaan
surface mail pos biasa
surname nama keluarga
surprised heran; terkejut
surprising mengherankan
surroundings sekitar; sekeliling
survive, to selamat
suspect, to curiga, mencuriga;
duga, menduga; sangka,
menyangka
suspicion kecurigaan
sweat peluh
sweat, to berpeluh
sweep, to sapu, menyapu
sweet (dessert) manisan
sweet (taste) manis
sweet and sour masam manis
sweetcorn jagung manis
sweets (candy) gula-gula
swim, to renang, berenang
swimming costume pakaian
renang
swimming pool kolam
renang
swing, to ayunan; goyang,
bergoyang
switch suis
switch, to (change) ganti,
mengganti
switch on pasang; nyalakan;
hidupkan

T

table meja
tablecloth alas meja
tablemat alas pinggan
tablet tablet; pil
tail ekor

take, to (remove) ambil,
mengambil
take off (clothes) buka baju
talk, to cakap, bercakap; bual,
berbual
talk about bercerita mengenai
sesuatu
tall tinggi
tame jinak
Taoism agama Tao
tape (adhesive) pita pelekat
tape recording rakaman
taste rasa
taste, to (salty, spicy)
rasanya
taste, to (sample) rasa,
merasa
tasty enak
taxi teksi
tea teh
teach, to ajar, mengajar
teacher guru
team pasukan; regu
tear, to (rip) koyak, ,mengoyak
tears air mata
teenager remaja
teeshirt baju-t
teeth gigi
telephone telefon
telephone number nombor
telefon
television televisyen
tell, to (a story) cerita,
menceritakan
tell, to (let know) beritahu
temperature suhu
temple (ancient) candi; kuil
temple (Chinese) tokong
temporary sementara
ten sepuluh
ten thousand sepuluh ribu
tendon urat
tennis tenis
tens of (multiples of ten)
puluhan
tense tegang
terrible (situation) buruk sekali

ENGLISH—BAHASA MALAYSIA

test ujian
test, to uji, menguji; periksa, memeriksa
testicles testikel; buah zakar
than daripada
thank, to mengucapkan terima kasih
thank you terima kasih
thankful bersyukur
that (introducing a quotation) bahawa
that (those) itu
that (which, the one who) yang
theater (drama) teater
their mereka punya
then dulu; kemudian
there (out of sight) di sana
there (within sight) di situ
there is, there are ada
therefore jadi; oleh kerana itu
they mereka
thick (of liquids) pekat; kental
thick (of things) tebal
thief pencuri
thigh paha
thin (of liquids) tipis
thin (of persons) kurus
thing barang; benda
think (have an opinion) berpendapat
think (ponder), to fikir, berfikir
third ketiga
thirsty haus
thirteen tiga belas
thirty tiga puluh
this ini
though meskipun; walaupun
thoughts fikiran
thousand ribu
thread benang
threaten, to ancam, mengancam
three tiga
throat tengkok
through menerusi; melalui

throw, to lempar, melempar; baling, membaling
throw away buang
thunder gemuruh; petir
Thursday Khamis
thus, so begini; begitu; demikian
ticket tiket
tidy rapi; kemas
tidy up mengemas
tie (necktie) tali leher
tie, to ikat, mengikat
tiger harimau
time waktu
time (from time to time) dari masa ke semasa
times (multiplying) kali
timetable jadual
tiny kecil sekali
tip (end) hujung
tip (gratuity) hadiah
tired (sleepy) ngantuk
tired (worn out) penat; letih
title (of book, film) judul; tajuk
title (of person) gelaran
to, toward (a person) kepada
to, toward (a place) ke
today hari ini
toe jari kaki
tofu tahu
together bersama-sama; sekalian
toilet tandas
tomato tomato
tomorrow esok
tongue lidah
tonight malam ini
too (also) juga
too (excessive) terlalu
too much terlalu banyak
tool (utensil, instrument) alat
tooth gigi
toothbrush berus gigi
toothpaste ubat gigi
top atas

topic hal; topik
torch (flashlight) lampu suluh; lampu picit
total jumlah
touch, to sentuh, menyentuh
tourist pelancung
toward menuju
towel tuala
tower menara
town kota; bandar
trade (business) perdagangan
trade, to (exchange) tukar, menukar
traditional tradisional
traffic lalu-lintas
train kereta api
train station stesen kereta api
training latihan
translate, to menerjemahkan
travel, to berjalan-jalan
traveler pengembara
tray dulang
treat (something special) yang memberi keseronokan
treat, to (behave towards) memperlakukan
treat, to (medically) rawat, merawat
tree pokok; pohon
triangle segitiga
tribe suku
trip (journey) perjalanan
troops pasukan tentera
trouble kesusahan
troublesome menyusahkan
trousers seluar panjang
truck lori
true benar; betul
truly sungguh
trust, to percaya
try, to cuba, mencuba
try on (clothes) mencuba baju
Tuesday Selasa
turn, to (make a turn) belok, membelok
turn around putar, berputar

turn off mematikan
turn on nyalakan; pasang
turtle (land) kura-kura
turtle (sea) penyu
TV televisyen
twelve dua belas
twenty dua puluh
twin anak kembar
two dua
type (sort) macam; jenis
type, to taip, menaip
typewriter mesin taip
typist jurutaip
typhoon taufan
typical (characteristic) lazim; biasa

U

ugly hodoh
umbrella payung
uncle bapa saudara; pak cik
uncooked mentah
under di bawah
undergo, to (hardship) mengalami
undergo, to (repairs) menjalani
underpants seluar dalam
undershirt baju dalam
understand, to erti, mengerti; faham, memahami
underwear baju dalam
undressed, to get membuka baju
unemployed menganggur
unfortunately sayang
unhappy sedih
United Kingdom United Kingdom
United States of America Amerika; Amerika Syarikat
university universiti
unless kecuali
unlucky kurang nasib baik
unnecessary tidak perlu

ENGLISH–BAHASA MALAYSIA

U

unripe muda; mentah
until sampai
up (upward) naik
upset (unhappy) marah
upside down terbalik
upstairs atas; di atas
urban (area) bandar; kota
urge, to (push for) desak, mendesak
urgent segera
urinate, to kencing; buang air kecil
us (excluding the one addressed) kami
us (including the one addressed) kita
use, to pakai, memakai; gunakan, mengguna
used to (accustomed) sudah biasa; kebiasaan
used to do something dulunya; sebelumnya
useful guna; berguna
useless tidak berguna
usual biasa
usually biasanya; pada umumnya
uterus rahim

V

vacant kosong
vacation cuti
vaccination suntikan
vagina kemaluan perempuan; faraj
vague tidak jelas
vain rasa megah
valid sah
valley lembah
value (cost) harga
value (good) murah
value, to hargai, menghargai
vapor wap
various pelbagai; bermacam-macam; aneka jenis

vary berbeza
vase bekas bunga; vas
vast sangat besar
VCR VCR; video
veal daging anak lembu
vegetable sayur
vehicle kendaraan; kereta
vein urat
vendor penjaja; penjual
very sangat; sekali; amat
vest (undershirt) baju dalam
via melalui
video cassette kaset video
video recorder perakam video
videotape, to merakam video
view (panorama) pemandangan
view, to (look at) memandang
village kampung; desa
vinegar cuka
visa visa
vision wawasan
visit kunjungan; lawatan
visit, to pay a berkunjung; mengunjungi; melawat
voice suara
volcano gunung api
vomit, to muntah
vote, to pilih, memilih; undi, mengundi
vow niat
voyage pelayaran
vulgar lucah; kasar

W

wages gaji
wait for tunggu, menunggu
waiter, waitress pelayan
wake someone up membangunkan
wake up bangun, membangun
walk, to jalan, berjalan
walking distance tidak juah
wall tembok; dinding
wallet dompet; beg duit

W

want, to mahu; hendak
warm hangat
warmth (personal characteristic) keramahan
warmth (temperature) kehangatan
warning teguran; amaran
wash, to cuci, mencuci
wash the dishes cuci piring
watch (wristwatch) jam tangan
watch, to (look, see) lihat, melihat
watch, to (show, movie) tonton, menonton
watch over (guard) mengawasi; menjaga
water air
water buffalo kerbau
waterfall air terjun
watermelon tembikai
wave (in sea) ombak
wave, to lambai, melambai
wax lilin
way (by way of) melalui
way (method) cara
way in pintu masuk
way out pintu keluar
we (excluding the one addressed) kami
we (including the one addressed) kita
weak lemah
wealthy kaya
weapon senjata
wear, to pakai, memakai
weary penat; letih
weather cuaca
weave, to tenun, menenun
weaving tenunan
wedding perkahwinan; pernikahan
Wednesday Rabu
week minggu
weekend akhir minggu
weekly tiap minggu
weep, to tangis, menangis

weigh, to timbang, menimbang
weigh out menimbangkan
weight berat
weight, to gain bertambah berat
weight, to lose menjadi lkurus
welcome (you are welcome!) sama-sama!
welcome, to sambut, menyambut
well (good) baik
well (for water) perigi
well behaved berkelakuan baik; tidak nakal
well cooked masak
well done! bagus!; hebat!
well mannered sopan; halus
well off (wealthy) kaya
west barat
westerner orang barat
wet basah
what? apa?
what for? mengapa?; kenapa?; untuk apa?; buat apa?
what kind of? macam apa?
what time? pukul berapa?
wheel roda
when? bila?
when (at the time) waktu
whenever bila saja
where? mana?
where to? ke mana?
which? yang mana?
while (during) sambil
white putih
who? siapa?
whole (all of) seluruh
whole (complete) lengkap
why? kenapa?
wicked jahat
wide lebar
width kelebaran
widow, widowed janda
widower duda

W

wife isteri
wild liar
will (shall) mahu; akan
win, to menang
wind (breeze) angin
window (in house) tingkap
wine wain
wing sayap
winner pemenang; juara
winter musim sejuk; musim salji
wipe, to (blackboard) mengelap
wipe, to (hands, face) bersih, membersihkan
wire dawai; wayar
wise bijaksana
wish, to ingin, keinginan
with dengan; sama; beserta
within reason munasabah
without tanpa
witness saksi
witness, to saksikan, menyaksikan
woman perempuan
wonderful bagus sekali
wood kayu
wooden dibuat dari kayu
wool benang bulu biri
won't tak
word kata
work (occupation) pekerjaan
work, to (function) jalan, berjalan
work, to (labor) kerja, bekerja
worker pekerja
world dunia
worn out (clothes, machine) butut
worn out (tired) penat; letih
worry, to khuatir, bimbang
worse lebih parah; lebih buruk; lebih dashat
worship, to sembahyang, bersembahyang
worst paling buruk; paling parah; paling dasyat
worth, to be berharga; bernilai
would akan; mahu
wrap, to membungkus
wrinkle kedut
wrist pergelangan tangan
write, to tulis, menulis; karang, mengarang
writer penulis; pengarang
wrong (false) salah
wrong (mistaken) silap

Y

yacht kapal layar
yam keladi
yard (of house) halaman
yawn menguap
year, years old tahun
yell, to teriak, berteriak
yellow kuning
yes ya
yesterday kelmarin
yet (not yet) belum
you (familiar, friend, same status) engkau; kamu
you (unfamilar, formal, polite) saudara, anda
your kamu; kau
you're welcome! sama-sama!
young muda
younger brother or sister adik
youth (young person) remaja

Z

zero nil; kosong
zone daerah; zon
zoo zoo
zucchini (courgette) zukini